SIMPLE PRAYERS FOR MEN

DAVID E. SHELTON

Edited by
Stacie Floyd

WESTBOW PRESS®
A DIVISION OF THOMAS NELSON
& ZONDERVAN

WestBow Press books may be ordered through booksellers or by contacting:

WestBow Press
A Division of Thomas Nelson & Zondervan
1663 Liberty Drive
Bloomington, IN 47403
www.westbowpress.com
1 (866) 928-1240

ISBN: 978-1-9736-5378-3 (sc)
ISBN: 978-1-9736-5377-6 (hc)
ISBN: 978-1-9736-5379-0 (e)

Library of Congress Control Number: 2019901723

Print information available on the last page.

WestBow Press rev. date: 5/9/2019

CONTENTS

FOREWORD

This book is written especially for you if you've ever struggled because life hasn't been completely fair or because things haven't turned out as you had hoped. As the Editor in Chief of Prayerideas.org I knew after reading the first article by David Shelton in 2011 that David was a truly remarkable writer who would strike a deep chord of hope in the hearts of all who read his works.

David is the master of putting us right there beside him in his "nothing left" moments of life and then helping us move alongside him slowly but surely back to the God who has never left us.

Like you, David hasn't lived a charmed life. His devotionals show him screaming at the ceiling and pounding on the walls when going through the aftershock of a divorce. Even though David is a gifted musician and worship leader, we are shocked when he is unfairly turned down for music ministry jobs because of his divorce. We tag along with David as he struggles to find a job of any kind to bring in a paycheck, then is underemployed for years before finding a satisfying alternate career path. We are there when he loses court rulings and when he deals with unreliable business associates. We're also there during the moments when God draws surprisingly near, such as when his children teach him profound lessons or when he makes a prayer list that leads to the unlikely meeting with his amazing wife Kelly.

Like me, you'll love how David talks honestly and openly with God, telling God things we've all felt like saying. David doesn't sugar-coat his feelings or the toughness of life or offer us empty platitudes. Instead he provides us tipping points toward hope. These often come to David in the form of a relevant scripture that springs to his mind in the middle of the murkiness of life. Or through a song. Or through a decision to worship in the midst of crisis.

In every struggle David finds that one gleaming truth that we've all been hungry to find. And then he embraces it and helps us claim it for ourselves through a memorable prayer that brings us the power to face another day. No matter what.

It has been my pleasure to edit David's work for over six years. He has proven to be a distinctive voice, a true original who is honest, insightful, and generous in sharing his life with our readers. On top of all of this, David is also one of our most prolific writers who never ceases to amaze me with his scope of life experiences. Each devotional is gripping, Biblically based, and just the right length to read and savor during any busy day.

David skillfully and vividly draws us into his life's "Oh no!" moments and then takes us on a seamless journey toward his final "Oh yes!" moment of trust and hope in God. For all of these reasons, I am honored to write this foreword to this wonderful book that will introduce David Shelton's work to many.

Karen Barber, Editor in Chief, Prayerideas.org
Contributing Editor, *Guideposts*
Author of *Surprised by Prayer*

INTRODUCTION

It should come as no surprise that the Body of Christ is under spiritual attack. Broken people, broken families, and broken churches litter the streets and towns of America. Church members stand in amazement looking at the carnage. As I write this paragraph, the Church in America is down on one knee after being punched repeatedly. The enemy is assaulting on every side: abortion, crumbling marriages, teen suicide, abductions, murders, sex trafficking, and the list goes on. Now we must deal with a Church being polarized on the political spectrum by the very people who make up the Body. People on both sides are attempting to subvert the Gospel by making Jesus fit their side of the argument. This is an amazing tactic that the enemy is using with great skill. And we continue to fall for it.

Everyday life is no longer serene - if it ever was.

The foundational idea of this book is not to provide the answers, but to provide a reminder that the Answer is found in Jesus Christ.

It's the first week of August and I sit perched on the twenty-first row in the twenty-first seat of Pennington Field in Hurst, Texas. I'm a band dad. For those of you who don't understand, the Texas high school bands have found ways to bend the University Interscholastic League rules so that they can begin rehearsing before the football players ever strap on their gear for the first time. My mobile office has been between here and the Starbucks off Central Drive in Hurst, Texas.

At the time of writing this introduction, I've been the "band taxi" this week shuttling my two daughters back and forth from home to practice. One daughter is in the band, while the other daughter is in the color guard. My son is in college and may be buying his first car this week. My wife is starting her 20th year of education but is in line for a new job at a new school.

Why tell you all of this? These are historical markers. They serve to remind my family and close friends what was going on when I opened up the laptop to begin putting this book together. They are historical markers in my life. This week has been a roller coaster ride, but filled with much prayer:

- Prayer for my wife's new job
- Prayer for the girls as they go back to the jungle that is high school
- Prayer for my son as he picks a college, picks a major, buys a car, and searches for a part time job

All of these events point to the purpose of this book. *Simple Prayers for Men* is just that - simple prayers. Sometimes a simple prayer is all we need. Sometimes it is all we can muster. Though simple these prayers can be powerful and effective. This is not meant to be an exhaustive study on prayer, but rather a starting point. This collection is meant to provide anyone searching for the "where to begin praying" marker in life a place to stand, kneel, or lay prostrate on the floor.

The significance of each of the stories written is that they give you, the reader, a glimpse into my life to show you that life is real, even for a Christian.

So much has happened to shape the message of this book, from the initial email I received from Karen Barber to the words of James Robison.

Karen Barber is my editor and Editor In Chief for the website, www.prayerideas.org. The website, home to *Prayer Igniters*, is a place where anyone can find guidance in praying for many different situations. Karen has been a faithful supporter and encourager, and was the first person outside of my family to tell me that she liked what I was writing. Karen first read my material that was part of an email to a good friend. *Prayer Igniters* was looking for writers for their new online project and, based on the encouraging email to a friend we have in common, Karen asked me to come on board to write prayer ideas for others. That was 2011. It was her blessing that I needed and received to start this project.

In 2017 I sat in the *Life Today* studios and listened as James Robison looked in my direction. I'm not sure if he looked straight at me, but I felt that James looked at me as he spoke the words, "The Father loves you." I still cling to that moment. I still cling to the words that pierced my soul. I wrote an actual snail mail letter to James and he read it not long after he spoke those words. I was hurting and feeling abandoned by the denomination I grew up in. For the first time in my life someone apologized to me that I had been put on the bench by the only denomination I had known for over forty years. James Robison is the spiritual leader who stepped up and on behalf of the denomination apologized. He also encouraged me that God was not through with my life. God had some "amazing" things to do in my life. It was not time to quit. So, to James I say, this is me not quitting.

As I grappled with my 50th birthday I heard a sermon from Pastor Wade McHargue. In his sermon, Pastor Wade said that "Believe" is the bullseye of prayer. I could not agree more. On that day I needed to hear his words. Pastor Wade encouraged the congregation in that church by stating that there is a need to believe in the God of this universe as we pray to him. Not so that he will be at our beck and call, but so that we show others our faith and trust in the God who does the miraculous, the unimaginable, the unbelievable, the unfathomable and "far more than we could ever hope or imagine." This book is my encouragement to you the reader to believe.

When you pray, pray in belief that God is who he says he is. Believe that God can do what he says he can do. Understand that he is a good father and that his promise to never leave or forsake us is true. He is the God you can trust.

These *Simple Prayers for Men* are the foundation for a spiritual journey. This journey has been full of the good, the bad, the evil, and the miraculous. It is my journey. It is my hope that the path I have walked will provide some insight into the steps you are traveling. Maybe my experiences will help you through yours. Ultimately, I hope that you pray the prayers found in this book and speak to the God of Heaven who hears and answers prayer.

This journey would not be complete without the help of others along the way: John Frank Reeve, Joe Warner, Kevin Gray, Joe Barrington, David Rotermund, Terry Lincecum, Jeremy Edgar, Don Owens, and Roger Fankhauser. My circle of friends who pray for me, encourage me, and help me sharpen iron against iron.

The following people have also had a hand in helping me write this book:

- Dr. Calvin Miller: You have left this world for the presence of God, but thank you for investing in me during our years together at Southwestern Baptist Theological Seminary. Thank you for inspiring me to write my thoughts down and leave room for places where I didn't have words, and to cut down the use of words that end in "ly." I will always treasure my autographed copy of "Walking With the Angels" that you signed at the end of class. I have passed it on to my son.
- Michael, Megan and Emily Shelton, my kids who have the weirdest dad on the planet and are proud of that fact. I will always love you, no matter what. When your children come along I promise to continue mispronouncing words (a la Bugs Bunny), sing silly wake up songs, and tell them stories that I can neither confirm nor deny.
- Revis and Sheila Shelton, my parents, who have loved and encouraged me all along the way. Thanks for being the original members of my fan club.
- Patty Casper, my mother-in-law who is the best in the world and always reminds me to "give yourself a yay!"

- My wife, Kelly, who believed in me when I didn't. The girl from Baltimore that met me in Romania, married me in Florida and moved to Texas to be with me; I love you...just because.
- Jesus of Nazareth. The Christ. The Son of the Living God who had mercy on me. Thank you. This book is because of what you have done in my life. May you do so much more in the lives of others for the glory of your name.

THE SECRET TO PRAYER

Hey! You made it! Glad you are here. I was wondering when you would drop in. So, have a seat, grab a fresh cup of coffee, and a notebook. While I have been waiting, much more thinking and processing has gone through my brain about what to say. So – ahem - here we go.

Ready?

Ok. A sip of my coffee first…aaaaahhhhhh. Much better.

The secret to prayer is…

There is no secret.

Boom! There you go. Problem solved! I'm glad we had this chat.

Huh? What did you say? That's it? Yeah, that's it. There is no secret to prayer in the Christian life.

Wait, where are you going?

Ok, calm down and sit back down.

Look, I have searched for a number of years to find out what secret code, password, prayer format, prayer position, or what posture, prayer blanket, shawl or towel I need so I can unlock the code to break through to Heaven and get God on the other end of the line so he can hear my impassioned plea for him to do what I believe needs to be done. After all, this is a crisis! Well, in my eyes it may be.

Or maybe we all just need to calm down and remember that God is God. A holy and righteous God who manages the universe that is held in his hand.

What I have discovered is that there is nothing we can do, say, put on, or contort our bodies to do so that God drops what he is doing in the throne room of heaven and gives us his full, undivided attention. We already have that. He is already waiting to hear from us. As John Eldredge likes to remind us "There is a way things work."

> "*The LORD is far from the wicked, but he hears the prayer of the righteous.*" (Proverbs 15:29 NIV)

The righteous are not the people who will say, "I have never done anything wrong." The righteous are the people who will say, "I have been redeemed and made righteous in Christ." These are the people from whom God loves to hear.

One prayer God always hears is the sinner's repentant prayer. Turning from the sin in your life to God is a prayer he will never reject.

Back to my original thought: The prayers of those who are called by his name will be heard. We have this in writing:

> "*This is the confidence we have in approaching God: that if we ask anything according to his will, he hears us.*" (1 John 5:14 NIV)

This is not a blanket covering that says anything we ask for we get. No, the words "according to his will" keep this promise in perspective. So, are we actively praying for God's will to be done in our lives? Are we praying to be walking in step with God, with who he is and what he is ordaining us to do? If not, this may be a place to start in prayer.

The first step in praying is to actually pray. Simple concept, I know, but many folks looking for the magic formula to connecting with God don't understand that prayer is simple communication with the only God who hears and sees us.

Jesus encouraged prayer and taught his disciples how to pray.

He taught them a basic prayer that still works today. It is a point at which you can begin to pray:

> "*Therefore, you should pray like this: Our Father in heaven, Your name be honored as holy. Your kingdom come. Your will be done on earth as it is in heaven.*
>
> *And forgive us our debts, as we also have forgiven our debtors. And do not bring us into temptation, but deliver us from the evil one. For Yours is the kingdom and the power and the glory forever. Amen.*" (Matthew 6:9-10, 12-13 HCSB)

The only true God of heaven and earth wants to have a relationship with you. You can start today with his prayer.

Thanks for stopping by. I'm going to go freshen up my cup of coffee.

Stay as long as you wish. Pray for as long as you wish.

I'm here to help, if I can.

Remember, you are loved just as you are. It's unconditional.

Grace and mercy are given for free.

There is nothing you've ever done, said, thought, or dreamt of that God cannot forgive.

You are loved.

NEED OR WANT?

When we go to God in prayer what are we praying for? Our wants? Our needs? Stuff we really don't need? Ask yourself these two questions: Am I being selfish with our prayers? If what we want is at the store with a price tag on it, why am I praying for that thing… when praying for others is so much more important?

In 1990 my dream came true. Well, what I thought was the ultimate dream at the time. It was time to buy a new car, my first brand new car, and I headed to the car dealership with one thought in mind: I will own a Chevrolet Cavalier. Yep, I had it all figured out. That was the car I could afford and I was going to own one. When I got to the dealership my life changed.

At the dealership, a place where my parents had traded cars for a number of years, the owner's son gave me this life changing sentence: "For the price of a Cavalier you could have a Camaro." The Chevy Camaro; my personal definition of a muscle car. The Camaro was sleek, powerful, rock solid in corners at 60 miles an hour, and a rocket sled on wheels. On top of that I could get the car in Metallic Blue.

A Metallic Blue Camaro.

My car.

Wow! I was in my twenty's and driving a sports car paid for with my own money.

I only kept the car for a few years. It was necessary to part with the vehicle I had dubbed the "Drum Machine" (because of its unique license plate "DRUMIN 7") because of changes in life. I missed that car and gave up hope of ever owning another one, until 2009 when the secret from the Transformer's movie was revealed. The Camaro was coming back!

So here I sit. The fifth generation of the Camaro has been reintroduced and I want one. Recently, my thirteen-year-old Honda Accord coughed up her transmission. Yep, the Accord has since slipped into a coma because she won't shift out of second gear on her own. (Here's where the prayer stuff comes in.) Being a believer in the power of prayer and the fellowship with God that it brings, I started praying for another car. I had to have another car. There is no way my wife and I can survive on one car because we go in complete opposite directions first thing in the morning. We have to be on opposite ends of the city at the same time. As I started to pray for another car, the Spirit convicted me on how to pray. I started praying for God to provide for our need. I **want** a fifth generation Camaro. God provided a 1993 Buick Le Sabre with sixty-four-thousand miles on it. Dave Ramsey would be proud.

I'm like most Christians in the West. I went to God and prayed for what I perceived to be an important need. God gave me an object lesson when I was praying for car needs versus car wants.

Let me introduce you to Wade and Katie. Wade and Katie, friends of my wife Kelly, were missionaries in a foreign country and posted reports about their lives in the mission field to their friends and prayer partners. The following is an excerpt from one of their posts. This is a clear example of praying for needs versus wants. This event occurred on the last night of a week-long mission trip outside of their village into neighboring towns:

"The last night we were there, it was the biggest crowd yet. The students boldly testified to those present to follow Jesus and how God has changed them. During that time of testifying we told people who were sick or in pain to come forward that we could pray for them. To my knowledge all were immediately touched by God. When asked who was healed by God that night about ten or so hands shot up for the glory

of God. We then called for those who were of the church or had given their lives in our time with them to come forward so that we can pray for them. About half came forward. We laid hands on them praying for God's fire on their lives, His glory to be revealed and for them to follow Jesus with all their hearts. I was touched by people as many times they would grab my hands and put them on their foreheads to be prayed for.... such a breakthrough we saw in the hunger and the spirit of fear being broken."

Another posting:

Yesterday, we (the students, Lalas and I) went to the hospital. I took Caleb who has so been wanting to come for some time. He was praying and praying for this time that "a hundred people would be healed!" I had to inform Caleb that I didn't think there's a hundred people in the hospital (then again maybe it's close). God indeed showed up and honored Caleb. He laid hands on an elderly woman on her chest who testified of pain (at that moment) in her chest and head. After he prayed for her, she said it was all gone and smiled! We said we wanted the truth, she said again, the pain was gone. Caleb smiled. We went to another man, Caleb prayed over him, he said the pain in his head went down. We saw a group of people who we had prayed over last week, they were smiling and testifying of what God had done, waiting to be released. One woman was beaming, it was the one Abigail prayed over, her leg was probably two times bigger last week now it was normal and she was full of joy, showing us by giving a little run. Another woman we've prayed over was also getting up and walking just to show us (she was bed ridden unable to walk for weeks before in chronic pain all pain left in prayer and hasn't returned)."

Let me ask the question again, "What are you praying for? Try the question this way, "For what are you praying?" The miraculous, healing power of God has not departed this world. The powerful prayers of the saints of God are heard by the One who created us and can heal His creation.

I can tell you that I am not praying for a Camaro. I am praying for God to work; to heal, to provide for our needs, to deliver us from evil, to give us opportunities to minister to others, and to continue His work on changing our hearts. After reading what God is doing in the country where Wade and Katie are working, I cannot bring myself to come anywhere near praying for a new Camaro. An inanimate hunk of metal, plastic and rubber cannot satisfy me. Seeing the power of God at work in the lives of other people brings the satisfaction that only God gives. Seeing God move and heal the sick and broken makes more sense than praying for something I can live without.

Wade made this comment about their students:

"The students as well saw many healings, their faith has increased dramatically. They are determined to see God be glorified in this way."

What about you? Are you determined to see God be glorified for answered prayer? Or are you determined to get what you want from God? Are you praying for you or are you praying for others with the assurance that God knows what your needs are and will "supply all of your needs according to His riches in glory"? (Philippians 4:19 HCSB)

The Apostle Paul gives a command regarding prayer, and it comes with a promise:

> *"Don't worry about anything, but in everything, through prayer and petition with thanksgiving, let your requests be made known to God. And the peace of God, which surpasses every thought, will guard your hearts and minds in Christ Jesus." (Philippians 4:6 HCSB)*

God's promises are true. He keeps His promises and none of them have been broken since the beginning of time. Notice that Paul doesn't say that our prayers will be immediately answered, but what is promised is "peace." The peace that comes from God and says, "Your petition is before God, you have poured out your heart to Him, and you know He will answer." With that knowledge we can go on with our day resting in His peace, knowing that He is in charge.

So what are you praying for? For what are you praying? Take a long, honest, and hard look at your prayer life. Look at what you are praying for and think about changing it over to "who" instead of "what."

Change "what" to "who" and begin to give God the glory for the great things He is doing. Begin to walk closer with God and someday Prayer Igniters may post your story about God's miraculous wonders that were performed in the lives of others because of your devotion to prayer. Walk closer with God. Get to know Him. You will then know what you are praying for.

"Father, I come to you now to confess that I have been the most important person in my prayer life and that I have not prayed for your power to be made known to glorify your name. Forgive me for not walking in the power that you have said is within us, the same power that raised Jesus from the dead. Show us your will in our lives so that we may be a witness to others that you are the same God now as you were in the days of Moses, Jeremiah, and Paul. May your Spirit rest on us and open our eyes to the world as you see it. In the name of your son, Jesus, amen."

Quotes from Wade and Katie used by permission. Their last name has been withheld to protect their missionary endeavors around the world.

SOMETIMES...NO

I asked God time and time again to save my marriage. He said "no."

I asked God to provide a different job for me several times over the past two years. He said "no."

I asked God to let me serve on a church staff again. He said "no."

As I write this entry, it is 11:30pm and I am seated in a hospital room at my mother's bedside. My mom is now twenty-four hours removed from open-heart, quintuple bypass surgery. We prayed that the doctors would be able to put in stents instead of having to go through bypass surgery. He said "no."

One basic principle of Christian prayer is to understand that God hears and answers prayer. One of the answers that He will give to you is "no".

The Apostle Paul had to hear "no" from God three times for the same prayer:

> *"Therefore, so that I would not exalt myself, a thorn in the flesh was given to me, a messenger of Satan to torment me so I would not exalt myself. Concerning this, I pleaded with the Lord three times to take it away from me. But He said to me, "My grace is sufficient for you, for power is perfected in weakness." Therefore, I will most gladly boast all the more about my weaknesses, so that Christ's power may reside in me."* (2 Corinthians 12:7b-9 HCSB)

Hearing God say "no" to your particular prayer is never easy. However, when God told Paul "no" He also said to Paul in verse nine that His grace is sufficient. First comes the "no" answer, but right behind is God's all-sufficient grace. When God says "no" accept the answer, but then wait for God's grace to take its place in your life. Don't run from God. Run towards God.

Although God has a very good reason for saying "no", you may never know why. Sometimes when God answers "no" the answer is related to something or someone else. The prophet Samuel delivered some bad news to Eli concerning Eli's sons. Eli's response was this:

> *"Samuel told him everything, hiding nothing from him. Then Eli said, "He is the Lord; let him do what is good in his eyes."* (1 Samuel 3:18 NIV84)

This was devastating news to Eli, but he did not run from or blame God.

King David also experienced a dramatic "no" answer to prayer, yet immediately afterwards, he worshiped God. In Second Samuel chapter twelve, King David spent seven days in fasting and prayer prostrated on the ground begging God to heal his son. His servants were afraid to tell him when the child died after seeing how ardently he was praying that the child be healed. However, when David received the news of the child's death the Bible says:

> *"Then David got up from the ground. After he had washed, put on lotions and changed his clothes, he went into the house of the Lord and worshiped. Then he went to his own house, and at his request they served him food, and he ate."* (2 Samuel 12:20)

Do you see here that David went towards God and not away? David's son died. Instead of blaming God David decided to worship

Him. This is the response of someone in a relationship with God. This is not the response of someone who practices a religion.

To hear "no" from God is perceived by many people as rejection from God. God is not rejecting any of us when we pray to Him and He decides that "no" is the best answer. In the Bible, each time God said "no" He had a better alternative. Sometimes when God answers "no" we will never know why. Not in this lifetime. Understand that this only means He is asking you to trust that His grace is sufficient.

Paul heard God say "no," yet Paul still walked with God.

King David heard God say "no," yet he chose to worship the God who had placed him on the throne of Israel.

Eli knew God on such an intimate level that he accepted the fact that God does what is good in His own eyes.

God rejected none of these men. Instead, God used them to bring glory to His name. God does not reject you. He loves you. In fact, this is what He says about you:

> *"The Lord your God is with you, he is mighty to save. He will take great delight in you, he will quiet you with his love, he will rejoice over you with singing."* (Zephaniah 3:17 NIV84)

That, my friend, is **not** rejection. That is pursuit and acceptance.

When God provides a "no" answer to your prayer the first thing to do is to accept the answer. Every time God has said "no" to a particular prayer of mine I have found that I can only respond one way. I found the response given by Job to be the best response:

> *"The Lord gave, and the Lord has taken away; blessed be the name of the Lord."* (Job 1:21b ESV)

Job just found out that his children had died, the children he prayed for every day. He found out that his life was a wreck because he had lost everything. Yet, Job praised God.

In these moments I have had to learn to say with Job "blessed be the name of the Lord." It's not easy, but as stated above I have found the sufficiency of God's grace when I run to Him. Make time to respond to God. It takes only a few seconds to respond to God as Job did…"blessed be the name of the Lord."

Say the words out loud no matter where you are. I have found that speaking out loud the words "Blessed be the name of the Lord" does two things. First, I hear myself saying the words, and it brings me confidence. Second, I am reciting the words written in God's holy Word. They are His words. I am speaking God's Word out loud. I believe that by doing this I am proclaiming God's words to anyone who hears me, including the Enemy who seeks to destroy me.

Since those times when God said "no" in answer to my prayers He has still provided all that I could ever need or want. He did provide me with a better marriage than my first one by providing someone who loves Him first. I still have my job and have found his grace to be enough to go to work every day and do my best. I'm not serving on a church staff, but I am ministering to people every day. My ministry has expanded to include writing for the *Prayer Igniters* website and serving on the board of *Another Child Foundation,* a non-profit organization that serves orphan and Gypsy children in Romania. My mom is, according to the doctors and staff, doing well on her road to recovery. The bypass surgery has turned out to be the better alternative in helping my mom to live a long and healthy life.

When God has answered "no" to your prayer what has been your response? Do you understand that "no" does not mean rejection? Do you know how much God loves you?

God loves you so much that He gave His one and only son. Sometimes He says in loving kindness to our prayers a gentle "no." When that happens, I encourage you to stand with Job and say, "blessed be the name of the Lord."

Run to Him.

"Father I come to you now in my time of distress. I come to you with broken and shattered dreams. I come to you with my fears…all of them.

I come to you with the pieces of my life, and I'm certain several of them are missing. I don't understand why you didn't answer my prayer with a 'yes' answer, but I will still trust you. I will not run from you. I will stay with you and ask that you pull me closer to you. Don't let me go. In the name of Jesus, your son I pray, amen."

THE DARKEST HOUR

Time and time again we face these dark nights of the soul not knowing what to do or say because it seems that God is silent or absent. The same God who said "*I will never leave you or forsake you*" (Deuteronomy 31:6) seems to have left the room. You and I sit and wait for Him to come back.

Oh, come on. You know exactly what I'm talking about. That lonely hour of the night of life that seems to pass about as fast as watching grass grow. You've been there. I've been there.

How well I know the dark night of the soul. The pain; the anger; the resentment; the guilt; the shame; the disgust over your sin and those who have sinned against you; the sleepless night trying to figure out how you and your family are going to make it through the next hour, let alone the next day.

The pain is insurmountable, reality seems to hammer at common sense with a relentless fury, screaming at the ceiling only gets the nosey neighbors involved, and your friends…well, your friends say, "We'll be praying for you" and vanish until they need **your** help.

A stroll through the local Christian book store will show books filled with information on how to get your body and mind together for a better, healthier you, and there's nothing wrong with that. There are books that will inspire you with stories of other human beings and what God has brought them through, books on prayer to get what you want out of God, books on books of the Bible, and many more. I have yet to find one that directly addresses the dark night of the soul, with the exception of a book by St. John of the Cross. This book deals more in mysticism and self-examination, rather than the redemption found in Jesus who will bring you and I through this dark night.

What do we pray? How do we pray in this dark night of the soul? From the man in the Bible who dared to write down his feelings in these dark nights come the words we all can recite, and call upon the Lord of Hosts. Hear the words of the Psalmist, King David, and speak them in your dark night;

> *"Lord, hear my voice when I call; be gracious to me and answer me.*
>
> *My heart says [this] about You, "You are to seek My face."*
>
> *Lord, I will seek Your face. Do not hide Your face from me; do not turn Your servant away in anger. You have been my helper; do not leave me or abandon me, God of my salvation. Even if my father and mother abandon me, the Lord cares for me.*
>
> *Because of my adversaries, show me Your way, Lord, and lead me on a level path."* (Psalm 27:7-11 HSCB)

More words from the experienced King:

> *Be gracious to me, Lord, because I am in distress; my eyes are worn out from angry sorrow-my whole being as well. Indeed, my life is consumed with grief and my years with groaning; my strength has failed because of my sinfulness, and my bones waste away. I am ridiculed by all my adversaries and even by my*

neighbors. I am dreaded by my acquaintances; those who see me in the street run from me.

I am forgotten: gone from memory like a dead person-like broken pottery. I have heard the gossip of many; terror is on every side. When they conspired against me, they plotted to take my life. But I trust in You, Lord; I say, "You are my God."

The course of my life is in Your power; deliver me from the power of my enemies and from my persecutors. Show Your favor to Your servant; save me by Your faithful love.

Lord, do not let me be disgraced when I call on You. Let the wicked be disgraced; let them be silent in Sheol. Let lying lips be quieted; they speak arrogantly against the righteous with pride and contempt.

How great is Your goodness that You have stored up for those who fear You and accomplished in the sight of everyone for those who take refuge in You. You hide them in the protection of Your presence; You conceal them in a shelter from the schemes of men, from quarrelsome tongues. May the Lord be praised, for He has wonderfully shown His faithful love to me in a city under siege." (Psalm 31:9-21 HCSB)

My place is to sit on the bridge of the second floor landing and pray this prayer over the entire house and my family. I wait for everyone to go to sleep and then I climb the stairs to get to what I believe is to be the center of the house. The bridge connects the two sides of the second floor and gives me a vantage point to see almost all of the rooms of the house. This is my place to sit in figurative sackcloth and ashes before the Lord. This is where I want to hear from Him and plead for my family.

This is not easy. This is not over in one night. I pray that this is for you and me a place to start. Trust me, after the first night of prayer and nothing is heard from God, giving up will more than enter your mind. The desire to give up will try and convince you to put the house on the market tomorrow. The desire to run away will come along and say, "Come with me." Don't go. Face the cross. Pray again. Grab ahold of the altar of heaven and refuse to let go until you are heard.

Maybe some of you are like me: when I am in that dark night, I want to be alone. I want to sit in figurative sackcloth and ashes, and I want people to leave me alone. (Yes, I see those hands raised in agreement.) We can't sit in sackcloth and ashes forever. We have to get back up and get back to life. One of the things that I do is to put my headphones on and get back to a sermon podcast from my list of teachers and pastors. One pastor who deals with the dark night of the soul in detail is Matt Chandler. I have found his sermons to be timely and appropriate. Please read the following excerpt from one of Matt's sermons. I believe you will find it encouraging and necessary.

I leave you with these words from Matt based on Matthew 11:28 where Jesus says:

> *"Come unto me, all you who are weary and burdened..."*

Please read them carefully and let them sink in:

From Matt Chandler, Lead Pastor of The Village Church in Flower Mound, Texas, "Prayer – A Call to Pray Part One, January 1, 2012:

"But the invitation itself is profound, because what we do in our culture, more often than not, is go, 'Look bro, you've got some people skills issues. Go to some sort of program, go to some sort of group, go to some sort of place and figure out how to interact on a level that's acceptable. And then you and I are cool.' Or there's: 'You're just a little too bitter for me. You're always complaining, always pointing out what's wrong and unable to rejoice in what's right. Why don't you go get better at that, and then we can do life.'

"But that's not what Jesus is doing here. No, it's, 'Come to Me. Are you a train wreck? Come here. Are you broken? Are you stuck in lust? Are you stuck in anger? Are you stuck fear? Get over here."

"And then there's this great exchange occurring. 'You come to Me with your weariness, you come to Me with your labor and I will give to you in turn rest. I will give to you peace. You give to Me the struggle, and I'll give to you rest. Get in here. Come over here."

"You've got to hear this invitation as it relates to prayer. Because the invitation isn't, 'Start doing what's right.' The invitation is, 'Come to Me. You're not doing what's right.' So the solution to what ails us, what weighs heavy on us and what exhausts us is not us trying harder at overcoming those things, but it's rather us coming to Jesus, walking with Jesus, being in a relationship with Jesus that overpowers our affection for the struggle. So I think it's really important for you to dial in and understand that, when it comes to sin, loneliness and despair, the way we get out from under those things isn't to work really hard to not be struggling with those things anymore. But we really need to use our energy and vitality to chase after, to know and to see Jesus as more lovely than those things. And then as Jesus becomes more lovely, these things lose their power. As Jesus becomes more spectacular, why would you choose a lesser joy over a greater joy? It becomes a delight issue."

"Come to Me," He says. "Are you busted up? Are you broken? Get in here. Get over here."

"So if you're here today and you're just like, 'Man, I just don't know if church is for me, because of this, because of this, because of this. . .' Jesus is going, 'Oh, you're all jacked up? Oh, it's for you. You're a mess and can't figure it out? Come on in here. Give it to Me, and I'll give you rest. Give it to Me, and I'll give you peace. Give it to Me, and I'll soothe your soul. Get in here."

The darkest hour of the night is the best time to go to the Scripture for a prayer to get through this dark time. This Psalm can help as you pray:

"The Lord is my shepherd; there is nothing I lack.

He lets me lie down in green pastures; He leads me beside quiet waters.

He renews my life; He leads me along the right paths for His name's sake.

Even when I go through the darkest valley, I fear no danger, for You are with me;

Your rod and Your staff— they comfort me.

You prepare a table before me in the presence of my enemies;

You anoint my head with oil; my cup overflows.

Only goodness and faithful love will pursue me all the days of my life,

and I will dwell in the house of the Lord as long as I live." (Psalm 23 HCSB)

THE DARK NIGHT

(Yes, these two chapters are similarly titled. As a Christian we sometimes deal with a deepening darkness that settles over our lives because the battle intensifies during the war. Remember that we are fighting against unseen powers, not against other humans. Sometimes our darkest hours turn into darkest nights. The second of these articles was written a year after the first.)

Are you at that point? The point where there is nothing left? You've screamed at the ceiling, you've pounded the walls of the rat-trap that barely passes for an apartment calling out to God asking for the exact reason why your marriage failed. You sat staring into the night sky wondering how a God who knows every name of every star you see couldn't hold your marriage together. You have recounted your story time and time again of being served with those papers and the embarrassment, shame, and misery they have brought. You have told your story to strangers in the hopes of finding answers. You have spent sleepless nights wondering how this could have happened and what to do next.

Begin by entertaining the thought that God was with you and that your questions, doubts, and moments of emptiness were the start of a prayer dialogue with Him. Why? Because King David wrote:

> *"God is near the brokenhearted; He saves those crushed in spirit."* (Psalm 34:18 HSCB)

I have to go to God and ask for help, even the help to believe, because I cannot do this on my own. I get down, despondent, troubled, perplexed, agitated, and angry. In those moments I have to summon the courage to say these words:

> "*The Lord gives and the Lord takes away. Blessed be the name of the Lord.*" (Job 1:21)

These are hard words to say because there has to be a belief behind them that God is in charge and that I do believe in Him.

For years that are unnumbered, God has been telling us the story of His love. We have read of His might, works, wonders, and love. We may believe that there is a God who has, can, and will do these things. However, the question is really one of: "Do we believe God?" Not, "Do we believe in God?" but do we *believe Him*?

Nothing surprises God. Your situation in life did not catch God off guard. He didn't walk out of the room to get a cup of coffee, walk back into the room, find out what happened to you after the fact, then smack His forehead and start formulating a plan to dig you out of the hole you find yourself in. He didn't start chastising the guardian angel corps for dropping the ball while He was out of the room. He is in the same place for your problem that He was when His own Son died: on His throne.

Do you really believe God knows you exist? Do you still believe that He has a plan for your life? Do you understand that this is not the end?

Wait. What was that? Failure? You? Your failures pale in comparison to more notable people who have failed. Moses killed a man with his bare hands. Peter denied Jesus three times. Paul murdered those whom he later came to call "brother" and "sister." You're playing Class "A" baseball compared to just these three and there are more. The Bible contains sixty-six books of people who were failures and all of them are loved ferociously by God. He loves you with the same ferocity.

All of these years later following the collapse of my first marriage, even as I write this, I fear failing my wife, Kelly, and my kids. God said don't fear.

> *"For God has not given us a spirit of fearfulness, but one of power, love and sound judgment."* (2 Timothy 1:7)

Do **I** believe God? I have to. I have nothing else. Believe ***in*** God. Now is the time to run **to** God, not the other way around. Now is the time to deepen your relationship with God, not walk away from God.

There's the crux of the matter: getting to know God. We thought we knew God. I have heard the story of an interview conducted with Billy Graham where he was asked if he could go back in time, what one thing in his life would he change? Graham's answer: to know Christ better.

If the great pastoral icon of our time says that he believes that a better walk with Christ is the one thing he would change about his life, where does that leave you and me? Here is a man who has proclaimed the Gospel to millions, who has read and studied the Bible more than most men ever will, who has written books about knowing God, and yet he desires to know God more.

"Get to know God." If we know God better, we will believe in Him. We will trust Him. Again, I ask you the question: Do you believe ***in*** Him?

Take comfort in the words of Christ:

> *"Your heart must not be troubled. Believe in God; believe also in Me. In My Father's house are many dwelling places; if not, I would have told you. I am going away to prepare a place for you. If I go away and prepare a place for you, I will come back and receive you to Myself, so that where I am you may be also. You know the way where I am going."* (John 14:1-4 HCSB)

In 2007 God introduced me to a wonderful woman named Kelly and we were married in 2008. From the very beginning of our relationship Kelly and I have had to call upon God to show us that He is still involved and interested in our lives. We made a point in prayer to ask God to show Himself evident in the situation we found ourselves in. Kind of a "Where are You, God?" moment. God answered.

Right before our marriage, Kelly was searching for a job in Texas. It was a tremendous task to try and search for a job when she lived fifteen-hundred miles away. Kelly had applied to several school districts around the Dallas/Fort Worth area but had not received any replies. It was imperative that Kelly find a job because the house we had just purchased, which we felt God had provided and in which I was now living, was only affordable if we had a two-income budget. We reached the "fervent prayer" stage when Kelly, my folks, and my kids all converged in a visit to the new house. We had begun praying in earnest about a teaching job the Saturday before Kelly's arrival. "God, Kelly needs a job, like now! Where are You in this?"

Kelly arrived in town on Sunday. On Monday she received a phone call on her cell phone from the Burleson Independent School District. The Human Resources representative said, "We received your application and would like to set up a phone interview." Kelly eagerly replied, "How about I come down to Burleson since I arrived in Fort Worth yesterday?"

Where was God? Right there and in charge. He had Kelly's job set up. He had the interview set up. He had her flight to Fort Worth set up. Even though we felt as though the situation was dire, God showed up and showed His majesty and power.

Maybe you have faced the desperate moments of life. You feel all alone. In those quiet moments of desperation, I have breathed a silent prayer under my breath that mirrors the plea of a father seeking help from Jesus: "*I believe; help my unbelief.*" (Mark 9:24) The Master, full of compassion and mercy, gives freely from the abundance He alone supplies: Grace. Overwhelming and free. The Savior understands and loves you beyond your wildest imagination.

There is no right or wrong way to pray to God. Make it a conversation. Even through tears and sobbing He understands. Through standing or sitting, walking or driving, in the morning or late at night God hears and, yes, answers prayer.

"Father, even when we feel broken and question our faith, make us one with you. Heal our broken hearts; put them back together as only you can. Forgive our unbelief and be near to our broken hearts. In Your Son's name, amen."

HEALING FOR A CHILD

Here in the stillness of the night I sit at my trusty laptop and write these words to you as two parents watch their outgoing and precocious fourth grade daughter battle for her life after contracting a life threatening case of E Coli. Can you imagine being these parents rushing to the emergency room because your daughter is not getting over the stomach virus the doctor previously thought she had? Subsequent tests now show E Coli and things just went from bad to worse as her body went into shut-down mode to battle the invading disease.

Have you stood in that room? Have you stood by that bed and held the hand of that child as he battles for his life? Have you been so exhausted that you're not sure what day it is because there are too many days to number since you entered the ER pleading for someone to help your child? I've been there because I was once the child in the bed.

My mom was the mother running into the ER asking for anyone to help her baby who was barely conscious and near death. My dad recounts a story of going into my room and picking me up from the crib. Dad said that it was a terrible experience because I was blue, and he wasn't sure I was still alive. I was alive, but barely.

One doctor told my mom that I would not live past age five. My mom gave me to God and asked that my life be spared. After I turned five and became sick again, she spent many sleepless nights wondering if that particular night was my last night.

I spent my share of time in the hospital in which the doctors were finally able to reach the conclusion that I was hypoglycemic. I would blow through all of my energy and my body would give out. From infancy to my pre-teen years I battled this unknown condition, and spent many nights in a hospital bed with doctors speculating as to the cause. When I burn through carbohydrates, my body goes into a reboot mode. I get nauseous, and then I want to go to sleep. A sports rehydration drink has enough electrolytes to help the reboot and get me back to normal. To this day I still must be aware of eating enough replacement carbs to keep me at "normal."

My parents have been through long hours in the ER and hospital visits not knowing what was wrong with me. I'm sure that if you had asked them, mom and dad would have voted to skip those particular experiences in their lives.

How could God let this happen?

Is your brain screaming to the heavens in hopes that your prayer makes it past the ceiling tiles, and some benevolent, all-powerful being will grant your wish? That's not God. That's not the God of the Bible. That's not the God who loves you above all the rest of His creation.

Jehovah Raphe is the God who heals. His Son, Jesus, healed many while He ministered on this earth. Because of this we don't give up…we glorify God. We call on Him.

> *"Is anyone among you sick? Let him call for the elders of the church, and let them pray over him, anointing him with oil in the name of the Lord."* (James 5:14 ESV)

> *"Bless the Lord, O my soul, and forget not all his benefits, who forgives all your iniquity, who heals all your diseases."* (Psalm 103:2-3 ESV)

> *"O Lord my God, I cried to you for help, and you have healed me."* (Psalm 30:2 ESV)

> *"If you will diligently listen to the voice of the Lord your God, and do that which is right in his eyes, and give ear to his commandments and keep all his statutes, I will put none of the diseases on you that I put on the Egyptians, for* ***I am the Lord, your healer****."* (Exodus 15:26 ESV)

You might be reading this and think, "What good can come from all of this disease and suffering?" I'll let a mom who is in the thick of it right now speak directly to you in her own words:

"When all of this is said and done, I hope that my daughters will have learned what it means to bless others. I pray they will look for opportunities of service throughout the course of their lives, and that they will always remember what it's like to be on the receiving end. I pray they will be gracious and kind just as you have all been to us. I know I have learned a lot myself these past few weeks, and I am forever changed. 'As each one has received a special gift, employ it in serving one another as good stewards of the manifold grace of God.' (1 Peter 4:10)"

The community of believers around the world have joined together to pray for this little girl and her family. Would you join us? Would you pray for this little girl who is battling for her life? Maybe this prayer is needed for someone you know. I invite you to pray this prayer and then for others that you know.

Maybe this is a prayer you need for your life:

"Father, we lift up this precious girl to you. All of these things have gone wrong inside of her body to cause her to be so sick. Your people come before you to lift her up and ask that You extend Your mighty hand and heal her from this disease that has attacked and ravaged her organs and blood. We know that You are "Jehovah Raphe," the God who heals. We bless Your name and remember You. We remember what You have done, how You have healed nations; and You have healed people. We cry to You for Your help.

In all the work that is done by the doctors and nurses, in all the medicines that are used, in all of the lives that she and her family will touch with this story, in all the prayer that is being lifted to Your ears by Your children, may Your name be glorified. May we reflect Your majesty. May Your mercy and grace be abounding. May this life be a witness and testimony of who You are and what You have, and what you will do. For the beauty of Your name we pray, amen."

Jesus cares for sick children everywhere, just as He cares for you. It's why He came to earth to die and rise again.

> *"But he was wounded for our transgressions; he was crushed for our iniquities; upon him was the chastisement that brought us peace, and with his stripes we are healed."* (Isaiah 53:5 ESV)

NEVER-ENDING EASTER

Another Easter season is past.

Some of you walked away from your first Easter service without that loved one. Some of you walked away from an Easter service trying to keep it together until you could make it out to the car before losing it because no one knows of the abuse you silently suffer day in and day out. Some of you walked away still trying to figure out how to make the house, car, and electricity payment this month.

Many people wander out of the Easter service and wonder if Jesus really died for their sins. They wonder about how a loving God could condemn people to eternal separation in a place called "hell."

Some people are experiencing what can be considered "hell on earth" because of horrific situations. Does God care?

Easter is over. So what? Who cares that so many lives are falling apart? Who really cares that so many hurting people walk in and out of the doors of the local church. Who really cares enough to make a difference?

Jesus does.

> *"I am the door. If anyone enters by Me, he will be saved and will come in and go out and find pasture. A thief comes only to steal and to kill and to destroy. I have come so that they may have life and have it in abundance. I am the good shepherd. The good shepherd lays down his life for the sheep."* (John 10:9-11 HCSB)

Jesus cares for you. Jesus cares so much that He gave His life in exchange for ours. He gave His life for every man, woman, boy and girl who has and ever will live.

Jesus loves you. It's more than a children's song, it's the only solid truth that stands in this crazy world we call home. It's the central theme that Dallas Willard points out in his book "The Divine Conspiracy." It's the heart of the Gospel.

From his daily devotion "Evidence of Jesus" Billy Graham writes: "There is more evidence that Jesus rose from the dead than there is that Julius Caesar ever lived, or that Alexander the Great died at the age of 33."

"So two contemporary theologians and speakers agree. Big deal." Is this your thought? The importance is that these two men come from very diverse backgrounds. One is the most highly recognizable evangelist of our time, and the other is a highly regarded Christian philosopher and author. These are but two intelligent men who agree on the simple premise "Jesus loves me and you."

How do we know He cares? How do we know He loves us?

> "*This is how we know what love is: Jesus Christ laid down his life for us.*" (1 John 3:16a NIV)

> "*But God proves His own love for us in that while we were still sinners, Christ died for us.*" (Romans 5:8 HCSB)

> "*Consider how the wild flowers grow. They do not labor or spin. Yet, I tell you, not even Solomon in all his splendor was dressed like one of these. If that is how God clothes the grass of the field, which is here today, and tomorrow is thrown into the fire, how much more will he clothe you – you of little faith!*" (Luke 12:27-28 HCSB)

You can pray this prayer right now:

"God, I need to know that You are here. Come into my heart and make me new. I need to know that You do care for me, and that you love me. Show me today. Let me feel Your arms around me. In Your Son's name I pray, amen."

You don't have to spend another moment alone. You don't have to spend another moment being afraid. You don't have to attempt to "hold it together".

Consider the words of this modern hymn. Let these words by your prayer:

"It's higher than the mountains that I face,
And it's stronger than the power of the grave
It's constant in the trials and the change,
This one thing remains, this one thing remains
Your love never fails, it never gives up, never runs out on me
And on, and on, and on, and on it goes,
Yes, it overwhelms and satisfies my soul
And I never ever have to be afraid,
This one thing remains,
*This one thing remains."**

Tomorrow you can get up and face the day because of this truth: the grave is still empty, Jesus is still alive, and He loves you the same.

(Publishing: (c) 2010 Bethel Music Publishing (ASCAP) / Christajoy Music (BMI) (Admin. by Bethel Music Publishing) / Mercy Vineyard Publishing (ASCAP) Writing: Brian Johnson, Christa Black Gifford and Jeremy Riddle. Used by permission.

A PRAYER FOR MY KIDS

Ok, parents of today's kids: it's time. It's time to put down your smart phone, put down your tablet device, put down the remote and **do** something **for** the kids. No, this activity does not involve cash, credit, or debit cards. Your job performance score does not depend on actually doing something for your children, and it will also not affect your credit score, bowling score, or fantasy football rankings. The lives of your children, however, depend on it.

What is this activity that I'm referring to? I'm referring to taking time out of your busy day to pray for your kids.

Here are some ideas.

Not much attention is given to the first chapter from the book of Job. In the very first chapter Job, a righteous man before God, prayed for his children. The description is given as follows:

> *"There was a man in the country of Uz named Job. He was a man of perfect integrity, who feared God and turned away from evil. He had seven sons and three daughters."*
>
> *"His sons used to take turns having banquets at their homes. They would send an invitation to their three sisters to eat and drink with them. Whenever a round of banqueting was over, Job would send [for his children] and purify them, rising early in the morning*

> *to offer burnt offerings for all of them. For Job thought: "Perhaps my children have sinned, having cursed God in their hearts." This was Job's regular practice."* (Job 1:1-2,4-5 HCSB)

Here is a father praying on a regular basis for his adult children. As a righteous man, a man who feared God, who the Bible says lived with perfect integrity, Job found it important to pray for his kids. I would imagine that his children lived with less-than-perfect integrity. Job had no idea if his children sinned or not. He did not take any chances and went ahead and prayed for them and their sin. Job made no assumption that his children were doing just fine without him. Job did not assume that his children had a party and did nothing wrong.

Sound familiar? Too many times parents give their children too much latitude, too much of the leash, too much freedom and the children do not know what to do with that freedom. The situation then takes a turn down the path to sin. Taking nothing for granted, leaving nothing uncovered by prayer, Job prayed for his children as a regular practice.

If God deemed it important enough to place in the Bible, then it must have some importance. God puts this in the context of the story of Job and places it at the beginning of the story. We should look at it from that perspective. You may feel that you are living an upright life. You walk the narrow path. You seek to follow the Lord with all your heart, soul, mind, and strength. The one thing that may be lacking is praying for your children.

Many people can quote this verse from the writings of the Apostle Paul to the Ephesian church:

> *"Children, obey your parents as [you would] the Lord, because this is right. Honor your father and mother, which is the first commandment with a promise, so*

> *that it may go well with you and that you may have a long life in the land."* (Ephesians 6:1-3 HCSB)

Does it not make sense that if you want your children to obey you, honor you, and respect you that you should spend time with God on how to raise them?

Let me put it this way: What do you want your answer to be when God asks you to explain what you did to raise your children in the fear and knowledge of the Lord? Do you give your children a reason to honor you? Do your children know that you are in a relationship with the God of this universe? Do you want your children to have a long life? I want to be able to say that I did all that I could and that I prayed for my children on a regular basis. Just like Job.

So what to do? Here is what Kelly and I do. We pray for the children every day, including two specific times a day. As a couple we pray in the morning before going to our respective jobs, and then at night before bed. We pray for their safety, for their rest, for God's peace to reign in their lives, and we pray for their spiritual safety. Yes, their spiritual safety.

Dear reader, Satan wants your kids. He wants to draw them away from you and God. Pray against the evil one and those assigned to your kids. That enemy is real and comes in many forms. The Apostle Paul said that we are at war in the spiritual realm and should pray as such. The battle for the lives and souls of your children takes place when you enter the throne room of the King and plead for His mercy to be shown in protecting your children.

My daughters know that some boy is going to come along and want to be the "boyfriend." The girls also know that daddy says he will bend in half any boy who breaks their heart. They know that I really can't do that, but my girls know that they are safe with me. My son knows I love him also, but I cannot translate video game lingo into this prayer idea for the average parent to understand.

As we are out in the world in our daily lives, we pray for the children as thoughts of them come to mind. A passing thought may trigger a thought of a certain child, which then leads to a short prayer for that child. Not hard or time consuming. In fact, it should be more the norm for every Christian parent.

What are your children worth? How much time? I always say to my wife Kelly that I wish I had more time with the kids. (For that I get a pat on the back and a reminder that she thinks I'm a good dad.) Since I cannot be with my kids 24/7 I pray to the One who is.

Pray today for your kids in the following areas:

- Pray for your kids to have a good day.
- Pray for God's peace to reign in their lives.
- Pray for their physical and spiritual safety. Take a stand and pray against the evil one on their behalf. If you don't, who will?
- Pray for the friends of your children. Maybe one of those friends will come over on a random visit and wind up giving their life to Christ. We had that happen earlier this year.
- Pray for the person God is preparing as a husband or wife to your child.
- Pray for God to go before your children to the jungle that is the school system.
- Pray that your children will not only know who God is, but that they will come to know Him.

1 Thessalonians 5:17 says: "Pray constantly."
Include your kids.

WHEN YOUR HEART FAILS

Where are you sitting now while reading this? Starbucks? Seated on the floor in your one-bedroom apartment? Maybe you're sitting on a sofa in Starbucks reading this from your phone. No matter who you are or where you are you will understand what you are about to read. Why? Put your hand on your chest. Feel that? That "thump, thump" is your heart pumping blood through your body.

In 2014 it happened. There's nothing quite like waking up to a racing heartbeat. I mean, how could I sleep with my heart pounding in my ears like that? I thought that my ear drums were being given a dangerous workout. This was especially concerning since all I had been doing was taking my Sunday afternoon nap. My heart seemed as though it pumped up and held for a second before pumping back down and continuing its rhythm. Oh, that will scare you all right, and I was plenty scared. I attempted to lay still and calm down. Getting calmed down was not going to happen.

As I write these words while seated in my son's gaming chair in the family room (just to let you know where I am) I don't feel 100%. All I have to do is think about it and it seems as though I can feel my heart beat up and pause all over again.

The heart beat: the pulse of our very lives, monitored with two fingers on the wrist or neck. Ninety percent of the time we pay no attention to the beating of our own hearts. Most of us don't pay attention until the beating gets louder or starts to fade. My heart had my attention in very short order.

How very quickly my thought turned to "What if I die?" There's no question in my mind; I have satisfaction and peace that comes from knowing Christ. I understand what the Apostle Paul meant when he said:

> *"For me, living is Christ and dying is gain."* (Philippians 1:21 HCSB)

If I stay here, if I see my kids grow up and have kids of their own; if Kelly and I get to buy that house on the beach and watch sunrises and sunsets together for many years to come; if I am useful for His Kingdom here on earth, if all that takes place and God allows it, then all will be for the cause of Christ.

If I die, well, that's easy. I go home. I will be whole. I will be at peace. I will be able to rest before Jesus makes all things new and this world is restored. That's "gain" for me.

In today's culture we are obsessed with eating healthy and exercise. I'm sure that there will be necessary changes ahead for me, but my health does not come from a lack of exercise or eating good food. This is my heart saying something is not right.

All of this had me thinking: what is the condition of my heart of hearts? What does God say about the heart of man? Here are a few of His thoughts:

> *"The **heart** is more deceitful than anything else, and incurable-who can understand it? I, the Lord, examine the mind, I test the **heart** to give to each according to his way, according to what his actions deserve.* (Jeremiah 17:9-10 HCSB)

Folks, this is God talking. These are His words. "The heart is more deceitful than anything else, and incurable." Wow. Furthermore, God tests the heart and gives according to the heart of man.

How is your heart now?

God spoke through King Solomon to pen these important words

> *"My son, pay attention to my words; listen closely to my sayings.*
>
> *Don't lose sight of them; keep them within your heart.*
>
> *For they are life to those who find them, and health to one's whole body.*
>
> *Guard your* ***heart*** *above all else, for it is the source of life.*
>
> *Don't let your mouth speak dishonestly, and don't let your lips talk deviously.*
>
> *Let your eyes look forward; fix your gaze straight ahead.*
>
> *Carefully consider the path for your feet, and all your ways will be established."* (Proverbs 4:20-26)

The words of wisdom King Solomon was handing down to his son and, ultimately, all of us, have much to say. If we keep the words of wisdom from King Solomon they can be a source of health for our whole body. A healthy heart is necessary to stay alive. The heart is the source of life for the entire body.

No pumping heart, no living body.

The rest of the body is dependent upon the heart moving the blood to keep life moving. Words of wisdom are healthy to a heart because stress can kill. Words that build up are better for a heart, rather than words that tear down.

Why does Solomon throw in speaking our own words? Jesus clears that up:

> *"A good man produces good out of the good storeroom of his* ***heart****. An evil man produces evil out of the evil storeroom, for his mouth speaks from the overflow of the* ***heart****.* (Luke 6:45 HCSB)

Do you, dear reader, see how the two are tied together? I explain this concept to my kids in this way: What we want to say or do starts in the heart, or the soul, and then goes to the brain which, in turn, instructs the mouth what to say or the body what to do.

Are you tearing down or building up? Are you being torn down or are you building up? As Jake Hess asked in the old hymn, "*How about your heart? Is it right with God? That's the thing that counts today.*" (Words by Bennie S. Triplett, 1954)

My physical heart needs some help. My spiritual heart needs more and more of God and His mercy.

Right now we don't know why my physical heart is acting up. The doctors are doing their thing and I'm trying to take it easy. My spiritual heart is getting equal attention. What wisdom can I apply to my spiritual heart so that it is healthy and ready to serve when called upon by God in a given situation?

While I'm physically not able to go to work, I can take time to work on my spiritual heart so that my soul is at rest with God. This will take some stress off of my physical heart.

How can we pray? By praying the Scriptures and believing the words we pray.

Join me as I pray:

"Father God, you have searched me and you know my heart. You have examined my mind and you have checked my heart. Lead me to have a heart and mind that runs after you. May my heart be a storeroom of good, and may I speak words that build up. Let your wisdom instruct me so that I may live a life according to Your purpose for me, that I may live long and run the race well. For Your beautiful name I pray, amen."

FINDING PEACE

A storm does not quite define the situations that we face in life. The storms of life are more comparable to a Category Five hurricane than a simple storm.

Have you ever sat in the still of the night, the room awash with ambient light from neighborhood street lights and the moon? Those nights when even in the stillness you can barely hear yourself breathe?

When I sit alone at the top of the stairs on those nights I ask God for one thing: *peace.*

But the storms of life try to blow away that peace.

Imagine with me: Outside the windows of life we are watching it rain sideways because the wind is blowing so hard. We are afraid of this hurricane that has blown up out of nowhere. Hunkered down in the house, a mattress wrapped around the bathtub we watch and listen as the hurricane blows. During a slight pause in the driving rain we venture into the kitchen for water and snacks. Movement outside in the backyard catches the eye.

You look again, and someone is lying on the hammock. The stranger is gently swaying back and forth oblivious to the wind, rain, and debris that fills the air, and the utter fear that grips you, me, and the neighbors. You grab a coat and ram your hands into the sleeves, pulling the coat around you without zipping it. Attempting to stop you, "Hey, it's a hurricane out there!" comes out of my mouth, but your ears ignore it. You stuff sockless feet into someone else's shoes because they are the first pair you find. Your mind races with "What idiot is outside in weather like this in **my** hammock?" You can't believe you find yourself opening the door, but for some reason you take a big breath as if to duck under the water. You are going to find out who this person is laying on a hammock out in the middle of a hurricane!

You're finding it hard to stand against the wind. The rain has picked up again and makes you squint to keep out what seem like buckets of water being dumped on you strangely from the windward side. Debris pelts you and threatens to tear holes in the coat that you are now wishing you had zipped up because it's hard to hold shut in this miserable hurricane. You must discover who this crazy person is. You struggle for footing against the wind, rain and debris. You finally get within a few feet of the hammock and are shocked at who is "hanging out" in your hammock.

That someone is gently swaying back and forth, eyes shut in pure delight, a small grin across his face. Then powerful eyes open and meet yours. A bare foot slows the hammock to a stop. You think the foot looks scarred, but in a driving rain and with squinting eyes you're not sure. As if to snatch you from the fury of the hurricane, a hand is thrust out into the wind, rain, and swirling debris to take yours. This is a hand you've never seen before but letting go of your coat for what seems like an eternal moment, you lunge with both hands to grasp that hand. You think that you have grabbed that powerful hand with a huge scar. This hand was thrust out with determination to reach out to you and grab you, pulling you in close and away from the hurricane. One minute the hurricane howls in your ears. Then - peace.

You are suddenly aware of your tight grip with both of your hands on His and begin to relax as you become aware of your surroundings. You are now staring wide-eyed at a hand strong and scarred. You gently caress the hands that blessed children and carried a wooden cross. You touch the nail print and water now begins to stream down your face, but not from the rain. In an instant you are strangely aware that the rain no longer soaks you, the wind no longer pelts you with debris, nor tries to take you off your feet. Sunlight comes from everywhere and the ground on which you stand is dry. There is a gentle breeze blowing which causes the hammock to sway.

You gather yourself and speak your simple prayer: "*I need Your peace.*"

Right there In the middle of the hurricane you drop your coat, kick off your shoes, and lay down on the hammock, nestled in the arms of the Savior who reminds you that He controls the wind and rain. He speaks into your life and reminds you of the words He repeated to His disciples over and over: "*Don't be afraid.*" (John 6:20 HCSB)

Jesus also told his disciples, "*Peace I leave with you. My peace I give to you. I do not give to you as the world gives. Your heart must not be troubled or fearful.*" (John 14:20 HCSB)

In the darkest hour of your hurricane can you see the Savior's hand? He is reaching for you. Grab hold of his hand with both of yours and don't let go. Then pray this simple prayer:

"*I need Your peace.*"

Why is Jesus interested in you and your problems? He loves you. In your grief over the death of a loved one, He loves you. When you lose your case in court, He loves you. When you think that you're going to lose it all, He loves you. He **brings** peace to your hurricane.

> "*He will be named Wonderful Counselor, Mighty God, Eternal Father,* ***Prince of Peace.***" (Isaiah 9:6b HCSB)

A PRAYER AGAINST INJUSTICE

I sat in my truck dumbfounded. I stared straight ahead as I listened over the phone to my attorney read out the judge's decision. My attorney was only going over the bullet points, but it was as though he was hammering me with a 2-pound lineman's hammer. I felt every blow.

We lost.

Not only did we lose, but we lost big time.

I could not believe that with the evidence we submitted, the testimony given, and the prayers we had prayed, the judge would rule against us. Where was the justice in this ruling? This was far from fair. How could God let this happen? Where was God in this judge's ruling? Didn't God remember all our prayers to Him that implored His divine intervention so that the ruling would be favorable? Did He not remember our tears, the late nights, and the hard work involved in gathering the evidence?

We wanted justice!

I wanted to cry after I heard the judge's ruling. I wanted to shout in anger. It was not a pretty moment when I finally let the anger out. I could not see God's hand in anything that was happening to us.

Have you had a similar experience?

Have you asked God for justice in your situation?

In light of all of that, let me take you to a garden. It's late. As we walk into the garden we notice three men seated on the ground underneath an olive tree. All three men look peaceful, resting in the defensive circle they had formed. Sleep has overtaken them, and now deep breathing is all we hear.

A little ways away we hear a voice. Someone sounds as if he is in anguish. "Dad, if there is any other way, please don't make me do this!" The struggle for justice has begun.

Now let me take you to a crowd on a hillside that overlooks the city. Hours have passed since we were in the garden. The crowd shouts jeers and insults at three men being given the ultimate capital punishment: crucifixion. We notice that the derogatory remarks all seem to be aimed at one of the three condemned men. We are shocked that the leaders of this mob are the local church leadership.

What has happened here?

Where is the justice?

The struggle for justice that began in a garden has continued through the night and has culminated in one man being punished to satisfy justice. "Justice must be served!"

Breaking the law demands a penalty. There must be a sacrifice to pay the penalty. So, we watch as one man pays the ultimate penalty once and for all. We watch as He struggles to breathe. We watch His body wracked with pain as it convulses against the wood to which he is nailed. We watch as the sins of every man and woman who has and will ever live are passed through this man. This man has never known any sin. Guilt and shame flood His mind. Every wrong committed, every thought, every word, and every deed of all of humanity pass through Him. We cannot comprehend the agony from the sin.

> *"My God, My God, why have you abandoned me?"*
> (Matthew 27:46b MSG)

This is the cry of the man in utter anguish.

The sky has become dark as the sun hides from the justice being served out on one man.

Finally, we hear words from this figure who is barely recognizable as a human being. His struggle seems to be over. He tells his best friend:

> *"Look after my mom."* (John 19:26-27 MSG)

With satisfaction and relief in His voice we hear his final words,

> *"Dad, I entrust you with my spirit."* (Luke 23:46 MSG)

> *"It is finished."* (John 19:30 HCSB)

Now justice has been served. The Law has been satisfied. The penalty paid. Jesus Christ died for all of our sins. He died the death that we should have died. He paid the penalty we all should pay. He alone has been served the justice required for the crimes we have committed against the Law, and the Lawgiver.

Friend, at the end of the day, you and I do not want justice as it should be administered to us. What we want is a watered-down version of justice that satisfies our own selfish desires. All we really want is payback, not justice.

Has the sting of the judgment against me gone away never to be felt again? No. I understand that God is in charge of justice. The payback I longed for was from my selfishness and not part of God's plan for my life.

With God planted firmly in charge of all things, including justice, His son, Jesus Christ, paid the penalty that justice demanded. Instead of the justice we deserve, we are granted Grace.

> *Indeed, we have all received grace after grace from His fullness, for the law was given through Moses, grace and truth came through Jesus Christ.* (John 1:1-17 HCSB)

What about you? Where is your heart? Do you want true justice, or do you want payback? I invite you to search your heart. If you feel as though you must pursue justice, I invite you to pursue the condition of your own heart first. Pray the following Psalm from King David before pursuing justice:

> *Search me, God, and know my heart;*
> *test me and know my concerns.*
> *See if there is any offensive way in me;*
> *lead me in the everlasting way.* (Psalm 139:23-24 HCSB)

Allow God to show you the areas of concern in your own heart. He may be leading you back to follow the instruction Jesus gave to us when He said: *"Seek first the kingdom of God and His righteousness..."* (Matthew 6:33a HCSB)

> *"Turn your eyes upon Jesus*
> *Look full in His wonderful face,*
> *And the things of earth will grow strangely dim,*
> *In the light of His glory and grace."*
> (Helen H. Lemmel, 1922)

A THANKFUL LIFE

Child custody battles, heart attacks, financial crises, the death of a loved one, persecution at work, no more Hostess Twinkies - all of these sound like reasons for not being thankful. However, the Bible says in 1 Thessalonians 5:18 (ESV)

> *"give thanks in all circumstances; for this is the will of God in Christ Jesus for you."*

The word "all" in the original Greek means "all."

Do I know your situation? No. Do I know where you are in life? No. You may be someone who lost everything that you own to a hurricane. You may be surfing the Internet on your mobile device because that's the last thing you grabbed on the way to shelter. I'm glad you're here. Give thanks because God is good no matter the situation. I know how hard life can be because the first paragraph is filled with situations I've endured in the past couple of years. I know hard it is to say "thank you" to God when it seems that there is no reason to thank Him.

Why give thanks in times like these?

Why not?

We have the very breath of God in our nostrils (Genesis 2:7) and the life we have comes from God. It is in the critical times that we come to understand that the stuff of earth does not satisfy. We were created to worship something or someone. When all the stuff of earth is gone we are left with a choice between the worship of another man or woman, or the worship of God. I would make a horrible god. So would you.

We are encouraged time and again to be thankful.

> *"Oh give thanks to the Lord, for he is good; for his steadfast love endures forever!"* (1 Chronicles 16:34 ESV)
>
> *"We give thanks to you, O God; we give thanks, for your name is near. We recount your wondrous deeds."* (Psalm 75:1 ESV)
>
> *"Sing praises to the Lord, O you his saints, and give thanks to his holy name."* (Psalm 30:4 ESV)
>
> *"It is good to give thanks to the Lord, to sing praises to your name, O Most High."* (Psalm 92:1 ESV)
>
> *"Enter his gates with thanksgiving, and his courts with praise! Give thanks to him; bless his name!"* (Psalm 100:4 ESV)

In the Scriptures, there is ***not*** a list of circumstances where giving thanks to God is optional. We see injustice, persecutions, erosion of liberties, disease, sickness and in all these situations, and many others not listed, we see opportunities to thank God for His goodness. His goodness in your situation may be your opportunity to be thankful for God for being God. He hears, sees, understands, and knows everything that is happening. He is with you.

Amid the worst fighting ever seen on American soil President Abraham Lincoln called on the country to pray to God and give thanks. Six-hundred-twenty-thousand people lost their lives from 1861 to 1865. Mothers lost sons, wives lost husbands, brothers and sisters were separated, families lost their fathers, and brother fought against brother. How could they be thankful in the midst of such a tragedy?

Yet in the United States of America, we pause on a Thursday of every November to give thanks as a nation. This observance was given to us as a national holiday by Mr. Lincoln. A portion of his proclamation read as follows:

"*Population has steadily increased, notwithstanding the waste that has been made in the camp, the siege and the battle-field; and the country, rejoicing in the consciousness of augmented strength and vigor, is permitted to expect continuance of years with large increase of freedom. No human counsel hath devised nor hath any mortal hand worked out these great things. They are the gracious gifts of the Most High God, who, while dealing with us in anger for our sins, hath nevertheless remembered mercy. It has seemed to me fit and proper that they should be solemnly, reverently and gratefully acknowledged as with one heart and one voice by the whole American People. I do therefore invite my fellow citizens in every part of the United States, and also those who are at sea and those who are sojourning in foreign lands, to set apart and observe the last Thursday of November next, as a day of Thanksgiving and Praise to our beneficent Father who dwelleth in the Heavens. And I recommend to them that while offering up the ascriptions justly due to Him for such singular deliverances and blessings, they do also, with humble penitence for our national perverseness and disobedience, commend to His tender care all those who have become widows, orphans, mourners or sufferers in the lamentable civil strife in which we are unavoidably engaged, and fervently implore the interposition of the Almighty Hand to heal the wounds of the nation and to restore it as soon as may be consistent with the Divine purposes to the full enjoyment of peace, harmony, tranquility and Union*". (U.S. President Abraham Lincoln, October 3, 1863)

How do we, with our nation in such unsettling times, pause to give thanks? We should follow in the steps of our forefathers and give thanks to God for our nation, warts and all.

Think about this: the stuff of earth belongs to God (Psalm 24:1).

Do you think about your stuff belonging to God? I used to not think that way, but Matt Chandler, pastor of The Village Church in Flower Mound, Texas, changed my thinking a few years ago. (For you resource junkies, I'm sorry, but I don't have this sermon referenced.) Because of that sermon you may hear one of my children thank God because chicken nuggets and french-fries taste good together. You might hear how good mashed potatoes and chicken on a stick taste. How good pancakes are. The savory goodness of peanut butter/ chocolate chip toast. We thank God for our home and everything in it - even the dust bunnies. It all belongs to God.

How do we do it? How do we live a thankful life? Here is my suggestion: Take a can of your favorite soda, and hold it in your hand with the bottom of the can in the palm of your hand. Next, hold the can with your fingers wrapped securely around the can. Then let go and balance the can in the palm of your hand. The can of soda represents whatever it is that you have in your life that is between you and God. The can of soda can represent whatever is holding you back from worshipping God. That soda also may represent whatever it is in your life that you are holding on to and will not let God take charge of.

Now, look at the soda can. Name the soda can whatever it needs to be. It can be pornography, obsession with social media, your child/children, your spouse, sports, politics, work, church. Now, balance the soda can in the palm of your hand and do not let any of your fingers touch it. Pray the following prayer:

"Father, I give thanks to You because you have what is in my hand. I'm letting go. I give it to You. I'm going to live my life with open hands so that You can take from me what will harm me, and place in my hands everything that I need for life. I give thanks that You are in charge and I am not. Thank you that a life with open hands waiting for Your blessings is far greater than holding onto the stuff of earth. Thank you. For Your beautiful name I pray, amen."

How do we give thanks? Give thanks with open hands. With

open hands we allow God to take out of our grasp the things that may harm us and replace them with things that may bless us instead.

Thanksgiving for the Body of Christ does not come one day a year. Giving thanks is for every day. Open your hands and give thanks to God because He is good.

ENDURING GRIEF

I don't know the level of grief you are experiencing. I don't know the depths to which you have fallen. I **do** know what grief looks like. So does the Savior, and He cares.

You may be the family from my hometown in 1978 burying your twelve-year-old son who lost his battle with cancer.

You may be the high school classmate of mine who buried her twenty-one-year-old daughter five days after that twenty-first birthday.

You may be my dad who buried his ninety-four-year-old mother after her battle with congestive heart failure.

You may be me several years ago going through the grief that accompanies divorce.

Everyone experiences grief. Grief touches every life on every part of the globe. Please understand that if you are currently experiencing grief that you are not alone, you are not forgotten, and you are allowed by God to grieve.

God understands this emotion. He has experienced it through His Son Jesus. When the prophet Isaiah spoke of Jesus one thousand years before Jesus' birth this is how he described Him:

> "*He (Jesus) was despised and rejected by men; a man of sorrows, and acquainted with* ***grief****; and as one from whom men hide their faces…He was despised, and we esteemed Him not.*" (Isaiah 53:3 ESV, emphasis mine)

Think about this: The Savior of the world, the "Lamb of God who takes away the sins of the world" acquainted with grief.

My high school friend lost her twenty-one-year old daughter in 2010. She is still grieving the loss of her only daughter. Many nights I have thought of what I would say to her. Many times I have wondered if the words I would say would be the right ones. The words of comfort I am reminded of are those spoken by Dr. Al Meredith, pastor of Wedgwood Baptist Church, after the tragic shooting on September 15, 1999, that left seven dead and seven wounded. When asked by a member of the media the question "Where was God in all of this?" Dr. Meredith gave the following reply:

"God was in the same place that He was when His own Son died: On His throne."

The best thing you can do in prayer is to go to God and acknowledge that you are grieving. Why? The Lord of Hosts, Creator of all, Lord of all, King of Kings, Savior and Redeemer is also a Friend:

> "*The Lord is near to the brokenhearted and saves the crushed in spirit.*" (Psalm 34:18 ESV)
>
> "*He heals the brokenhearted and binds up their wounds.*" (Psalm 147:3 ESV)
>
> "*The Spirit of the Lord God is upon me, because the Lord has anointed me to bring good news to the poor;* ***He has sent me to bind up the brokenhearted****, to proclaim liberty to the captives, and the opening of prison to those who are bound.*" (Isaiah 60:1 ESV, emphasis mine)

Acknowledge to God that you are grieving. Tell Him you are filled with grief. Tell Him of the sorrow, pain, suffering, loneliness, and loss you are feeling. Shout it, yell it, cry through it, write it down, type it out - do something to get it out. Tell God how you are feeling and why. Tell God what you are going through. Express your feelings to God. He is a big God and can handle you coming to Him through your pain and tears. Any of these avenues can be a way for you to pray to God.

I once told a grieving friend that I would take him to the roof of the hospital so that he could scream, yell, shout, bellow, screech, or whatever it was he wanted to do to tell God exactly how he was feeling. My promise to him was to guard the door and tell those who came to stop my friend, "It's okay. He's just venting." To the passers-by or those who came to stop him I would have said that this was a conversation between a man and God. A man who felt God should answer his prayer to let his days-old child live, and a God who would listen with love to a son He loved. Two weeks later I stood at the graveside where no parent should ever have to stand, and watched my friend weep uncontrollably as family and friends bid good bye to a beautiful little girl who will know nothing of this world.

In 1978 a family in my hometown buried their son. David was a year older than me. We went to church together and our families knew each other. This young man fought brain cancer heroically. The amazing story comes out of the night David's body died. The night of his death David's father heard the sound of footsteps on the roof of their home. That night a father asked a dying son, "Are you ready to meet Jesus?" A simple nod in response and the boy was gone.

Footsteps? Yes. Audible footsteps as though someone was walking on the roof.

Matt Chandler, Teaching Pastor at The Village Church, in his sermon series "Transitions," has suggested that we as Christians will not know the sting of death. I like Matt's take on this. Matt said that in the moment that we are to die, Jesus or an angel shows up to say "Hey, man. Let's get out of here." He gets the idea from Jesus in John 8:51 where Jesus says:

> *"I tell you the truth, if anyone keeps my word, he will never see death."*

I believe that night David did not see death, but rather the face of the Savior.

Are you grieving the death of a loved one? Take heart if that loved one believed in Jesus as Savior. Take heart for your own life. If Matt is right and, in that moment, your loved one did not see death but transitioned from earth to God's presence, think of what a wonderful moment that must have been! One minute you are staring your mortality full in the face, the next you meet the Savior face to face. "Oh, that will be glory for me…"

Accepting that death is not final separation but a mere transition, is a tough concept for some to accept. This point of acceptance requires a journey; but we do not walk apart from the Savior. He walks with us. In the last half of Hebrews 13:5, the Apostle Paul points out Jesus' words of encouragement:

> *"…for He Himself has said 'I will never leave you or forsake you."*

Jesus.
Here with us.
Emmanuel.
God with us.

Some months after David's funeral, his grieving mother said to my mom: "Don't take this wrong, but I wish it was your 'David' and not mine." Up to that point in my life I had been sick quite a bit. My problem was only hypoglycemia; nothing that measured up to the devastation of cancer. In her grief, David's mom said what was on her heart. My mom's response was a hug. When we make our final transition to enter into the presence of God I believe that His arms will be open and comforting; the secure arms of the Creator will wrap around us in an embrace that will bring final peace and relief.

In February of 2011 I went through the loss of my grandmother, my last surviving grandparent. Grief abounded. While I praised God that my grandmother made her transition from earth to the presence of God, I was grieving her loss because she loved me. She cared for me. She was there as a rock when I went through my divorce. She was a phone call away at almost any time. Only Bingo at the nursing home could interrupt our phone call. I can't imagine being my dad and saying good bye to the last surviving parent. In this grief my dad and I were reminded that "*...My grace is sufficient for you.*" (2 Corinthians 12:9)

I have grieved the loss of my marriage. I grieved the loss of the covenant that I thought was established. My grief was deep, dark, and almost all-consuming. I spent many nights sitting with my friend, John Reeve, in front of his chiminea attempting to talk through my grief. I cried out to God - literally. I cried out for help. Then I cried myself to sleep. In this grief I was reminded that "*My grace is sufficient for you.*" (2 Corinthians 12:9)

I don't know what grief you are going through. I may not be able to identify with your particular kind of grief. I do know this: Grief is hard. Grief can suck the life out of you. However, grief doesn't have to control your life.

Friend, there is no specific verse in the Bible for much of the grief we go through. There is no single verse for a parent who must bury her child. There was no class in seminary that covered what one should say to the parents of a child that has died. There was no seminar or practicum on grief and grieving. We do the only thing we know to do: turn to God.

Every year, as we remembered the of the 9/11 attacks on America, we are once again confronted with the grief that gripped so many that day, and the days and years to follow. Once again, the Body of Christ must remind those who grieve that in a time of grief, God is near.

If you feel immersed to the depths of grief please read these words again and again:

> *"I also saw the Holy City, new Jerusalem, coming down out of heaven from God, prepared like a bride adorned for her husband. Then I heard a loud voice from the throne: Look! God's dwelling is with humanity; and He will live with them. They will be His people, and God Himself will be with them and be their God.*
>
> *He will wipe away every tear from their eyes.* ***Death will no longer exist; grief, crying, and pain will exist no longer, because the previous things have passed away****.*
>
> *Then the One seated on the throne said, "Look! I am making everything new." He also said, "Write, because these words are faithful and true." And He said to me, "It is done! I am the Alpha and the Omega, the Beginning and the End. I will give water as a gift to the thirsty from the spring of life. The victor will inherit these things, and I will be his God, and he will be My son."* (Revelation 21:2-7, HSCB)

In your grief may you find the one thing that only Jesus Christ can provide. May you find that in Him is the path through grief that so many of us have walked. What is this that you are looking for, what we have found, and only the Savior provides? Hope.

Do you need rest from your grief? Then pray this prayer from the writer of the book of Psalms, King David:

> *"Rest in God alone, my soul,*
> ***for my hope comes from Him****.*
> *He alone is my rock and my salvation,*
> *my stronghold; I will not be shaken.*
> *My salvation and glory depend on God, my strong rock.*

> *My refuge is in God."* (Psalm 62:5-7, ESV, emphasis mine)

In your grief may I remind you again that God is near? He loves you. He understands. He was "a man of sorrows, acquainted with grief."

WE ARE THE BROKEN

I specifically give you a group of ragtag men who weekly get together to talk about life. We study the Bible, we pray for each other, we hold each other accountable, we are there for each other, and we support one another. We are "The Broken." We are "Men of Valor." We are the ordinary men you see walking around the mall, at the grocery store, drooling over electronics at Best Buy, dreaming of fulfilling that mid-life crisis as we walk through the muscle car section at the car dealership, and we're the guys crying over what's happening in life on Tuesday nights.

People today ask more and more what the solution is to our world's problems. I can tell you that it's the same solution that has been in existence for more than two-thousand years. His name is Jesus. How can that be? No one alive today has actually seen Jesus. No one alive today heard any of his sermons. No one alive today witnessed any of his miracles, let alone talked with anyone who was touched by him or what he did for them. No one alive today has any proof or evidence for Jesus' existence except that which is provided by the Bible and historical texts. Why should we believe in him? If you don't believe that Jesus lived, died, and rose again, then you can't believe that Alexander the Great existed at all. There is more historical proof outside of the Bible that Jesus existed, than that of Alexander.

What's the best way to see the evidence of Jesus in today's world? People.

I know Jesus was born of a Virgin, lived, died, and was raised three days later. I know that he is who he says he is: God. If he was not God, then we have no other explanation for how He is moving in the lives of these broken, sinful men I call "brothers" on Tuesday nights. You see, we are like most of you. We are welders, small business owners, retired military, stay-at-home dads, business professionals, bikers, hunters, computer gurus, and ranchers. We shake hands and we hug. We challenge each other. We shoot guns together. We eat roast beast together (elk, deer - you get the picture). We serve in our church together. We call each other out. We help each other out. We are learning that manly men fall down and have to get back up.

If I could give you a better summary, I would say this: our men's group looks a lot like the disciples that Jesus called. No, I'm not calling our group equal to the twelve men Jesus walked with, taught, and did life with for three years. What I am saying is that Jesus called the unqualified. None of the guys in my group (myself included) would think that Jesus might have looked our way and said "Follow me."

But let's look at the disciples:

- **Peter**: husband, father, fisherman and denied Christ three times (Matthew 26:69-75). Thankfully, Jesus restored him (John 21:15-17).
- **Matthew**: Tax collector (Matthew 9:9). Automatic outcast of society because he was friendly to the Roman empire that oppressed his fellow Israeli countryman with the overburden of heavy taxation to pay for the Roman occupation of Israel.
- **James and John**: also fisherman, brothers, and who had an overzealous mom who requested that Jesus seat one of her sons at either his left or right hand when Jesus finally ascended to power and ruled over Israel as King.
- **Thomas**: doubted Jesus had actually risen from the dead. He wanted proof. Jesus gave it to him (John 20:24-29).

This is just a sampling of the men Jesus called; rough, crude, mostly uneducated, and on the lower end of society.

But that's how I know Jesus is alive and lives in me. If he can take me, a sinner, a fallen, broken man and redeem me - and I am seeing him do the same in the lives of the men I meet with on Tuesday night - then how can Jesus not be who he says he is. We've seen answered prayer. We've seen unanswered prayer. We've seen lives get better. We've seen lives get worse. We've wrestled with the Scriptures and what God is saying in them to us. We've made realizations that iron does indeed sharpen iron, but it involves friction to do so.

The one factor that unites us is the love of Christ. We could not do life without the love of Christ. Why? The Apostle Paul answers this for us:

> "*Who can separate us from the love of Christ? Can affliction or anguish or persecution or famine or nakedness or danger or sword? As it is written: Because of You we are being put to death all day long; we are counted as sheep to be slaughtered. No, in all these things we are more than victorious through Him who loved us. For I am persuaded that not even death or life, angels or rulers, things present or things to come, hostile powers, height or depth, or any other created thing will have the power to separate us from the love of God that is in Christ Jesus our Lord!" (Romans 8:35-39, HSCB)*

If you are walking through life and believe that no one else has ever been where you've been, or lived through what you live through, I challenge you to find a church that preaches the Gospel of Christ. Inside that body of believers I'm sure you'll find someone who has been where you are, and they would love to encourage you to know Christ and how he can make a difference in your situation. I see it most every week when our group gets together.

If you're not sure, then pray this prayer with me:

"Father God, I need to know you are near. I need to know that I'm not alone. Please bring someone into my life who will show me your love and kindness, your grace and mercy, and your forgiveness. I am one of "The Broken." My life is in pieces and I need your help to find all the pieces, so you can put me back together. Help me understand that for every missing piece I can't find, you will make a new one to fit in its place. Give me the courage to reach out and ask for help. Make me your child. Be a father to me, and thank you for loving me when I'm convinced I don't deserve it. In the beautiful name of your son, Jesus, I pray. Amen."

WHEN TIME SLOWS DOWN

I never really had one of those moments where everything slowed down until November 1, 2013. A man I never met, and will likely never meet, fell asleep behind the wheel of his car that morning around 7am. His car crossed from the far right-hand lane across two more lanes of traffic, then jumped the curb of the median, rumbled across the twenty-foot-wide median, and crossed into oncoming traffic. I was in the middle lane of the oncoming traffic. The pickup truck about fifteen yards in front of me swerved to the shoulder to avoid the car that had come to a stop in the middle lane. I started to head left around the car, but the car suddenly turned straight into me before I could take any more action.

I remember saying "No!" right before impact.

I was in "protector" mode because my two daughters were asleep in the car. We had dropped off my son at marching band practice, and I was headed to the Quik Trip to put gas in the car. "No" meant, "you're not going to hurt us" and "I'm not going out like this." "No" was a statement. It was uttered in protest. "No" was a prayer. Not now, not my daughters, and not like this.

The air bag deployed with a ferocious force and punched me in the chest like a heavyweight boxer. I remember watching the hood bend up in front of me. My 1993 Buick Le Sabre muscled up and took this hit in the nose. I watched as the car gasped its last breath before coughing out its last rumble. I watched the air bag sag back onto the steering wheel from where it deployed and saw the powder-like particles float in the air after delivering the life-saving blow that kept me from hurtling into the steering wheel. My seatbelt had locked me down into the seat and I was going nowhere without the seatbelt releasing. To the designers and makers of the Buick Le Sabre: thank you. It worked.

It seemed like several minutes passed before my daughters came to the realization of what had taken place and what was going on around them. The impact woke them up and after taking in the scene they started screaming at me wanting to know if I was okay. It was at this point that life went back to normal speed. My ball cap and glasses were now in the back seat. The radio was still playing my favorite morning radio show and the slightly warm air was still blowing from the vents. Tears now flowed from my daughter's eyes as they took in the sight of their dad, bloodied and bruised having trouble breathing. The kept asking me if I was ok, and I assured them that I was. Good Samaritan's started to stop and check on us. I wasn't sure if the door would open, so I rolled down the window. Finally, I had the bright idea to open the door. When I got the door open and the air started to clear, I figured out that I needed to release my seatbelt. It was crushing me. Once it was unhooked, I could breathe a little easier.

For some reason I reached down and grabbed my phone and texted my wife, Kelly. I told her I needed help and for her to come. By the time she reversed direction from heading to work and headed towards the scene of the accident, all three of us had been put in neck collars and onto backboards to stabilize any possible broken or bruised bones. Kelly was re-routed to the emergency room in one of the hospitals in downtown Fort Worth. The girls were taken to the children's hospital a couple of blocks away.

When Kelly arrived, I finally cried. I sobbed and sobbed, not over the Dallas Cowboys windbreaker they had to cut off of me, but I sobbed because I could have lost my daughters. It all could have been so much worse. I did not know what shape I was in. I did not know if, and how bad I was hurt internally. As a teenager, I managed to put a hairline fracture in my sternum. Now, I was wondering if my sternum had more of a crack than a hairline fracture.

It was at the moment that Kelly took my hand, leaned over me and prayed. She thanked God that we were alive and that we were in the caring hands of the medical professionals. She prayed for God to heal whatever was broken and to bring peace to my mind. She also thanked God that my parents were already on their way to Texas and would be there in a few short hours.

Later in the day, according to the CT scan, the ER doctor informed me that I had only a chest contusion from the airbag. No broken bones, no sprains, and no dislocations. No serious neck or back injuries, and the girls were unhurt as well. I would find out six months later that I had jammed my ankle, and my tibia and fibula were slightly displaced. A sports medicine doctor got me back in alignment.

I have to insert a thought right here: I was not afraid of death. Death means that I get what I have asked for. I get to walk up to the Father and put up my hands. He will pick me up and place me on his lap, enfold me in his arms of eternal protection, and allow me to close my eyes and rest as I listen to His heartbeat lull me to sleep. No more contacts to put in my eyes, no more allergies, no more colds when the seasons change from fall to winter, no more battle with my waistline, and the list goes on. *"For to me to live is Christ, and to die is gain."* (Philippians 1:21 ESV). All those I would leave behind would be sad and would mourn. I would be made whole and I would finally be at home. It was not my appointed time and I am still here.

Since November 1, 2014, we've had more days that seemed so dark and we felt so far away from God. I would venture to guess that the majority of those reading this page have been there as well. I had to go back and read what I have written before on the Prayer Ideas website. I had to go read my own words of encouragement to others to run **to** God and **not** from Him. I had to wonder if my faith was enough to continue to believe in Him. Thankfully, the faith to believe comes from God and is not something we have to conjure up ourselves.

I always come back to the same place. I always come back to the place where God is enough and that none of what is happening has surprised Him or caught Him off guard.

Maybe this is you, dear reader, right now. Maybe your world seems very dark and you feel very lonely or separated from the Maker of heaven and earth. Maybe you need this prayer for your life right now:

"God, it is so hard to pray to you right now. I feel so far away from You, and I'm not sure if You can even hear me. I choose to pray to You despite my circumstances and how I feel. I'm choosing to run to You and not from You. I choose to believe that You have a plan for me, that Your arm is not too short to save, that You will provide for me as You promised, and that You will not leave me or walk away from me at any point in my life. Please forgive me for my sins against You. Please help me and show me how to trust You when it appears as though I can't find You. I choose to trust in You. In the name of Your son, Jesus, I pray, amen."

My daughters and I essentially walked away from the accident without physical injuries. The memories, however, still linger. Someday this will be a memory that we will talk about and how things changed from that moment on. Since the accident my youngest has attempted to encourage me that what I really need to drive is a full-size, crew cab Chevy Silverado. Since that time life has not gotten easier.

My life has become 2 Corinthians 1:3-7. I write to you, dear reader, because of the following words that have become my life story:

"Blessed be the God and Father of our Lord Jesus Christ, the Father of mercies and God of all comfort, who comforts us in all our affliction, so that we may be able to comfort those who are in any affliction, with the comfort with which we ourselves are comforted by God. For as we share abundantly in Christ's sufferings, so through Christ we share

abundantly in comfort too. If we are afflicted, it is for your comfort and salvation; and if we are comforted, it is for your comfort, which you experience when you patiently endure the same sufferings that we suffer. Our hope for you is unshaken, for we know that as you share in our sufferings, you will also share in our comfort."

SUFFERING WELL

Did you hear it? Oh, I'm sure you did. I heard it so loud that I thought that something popped like a barrage balloon from World War II. It was my wrist.

I had crawled into the back of my work truck looking for a data cable. After a fruitless search I started to back out. I put my right hand down on the bed of the truck, leaned my weight over on it as I have done so many times and POP! We will not delve into what occurred in the immediate minutes following this accident because God has forgiven me for the words I thought and said.

How about you? What has happened to you today or yesterday or last week or…whenever it occurred…that has caused an immediate shift in your plans, and could be, in particular, devastating? Was the car you were trying to sell side-swiped while sitting on the street? That was my car. Ready to sell, ready to get rid of and now I have to deal with the police for the hit and run aspect, and the insurance company for the claim aspect. Maybe you were knocked down by a cow and had both arms broken, and one elbow and wrist shattered. (Yeah, that one is real, also. It did not happen to me.)

How bad can it get?

Bad.

The real question is: What will you do with the opportunity before you to glorify God?

How the world sees the bad stuff in your life and how God sees it are two very different points of view. We know what the world says, but what does God say? Let's step back in time and hear the words of Jesus on the side of that mountain as He spoke to a huge crowd:

> *"You are blessed when they insult and persecute you and falsely say every kind of evil against you because of Me. Be glad and rejoice, because your reward is great in heaven. For that is how they persecuted the prophets who were before you."* (Matthew 5: 11-12 HCSB)

Consider what Paul wrote in his letter to the Philippians:

> *"Whatever happens, conduct yourselves in a manner worthy of the gospel of Christ. Then, whether I come and see you or only hear about you in my absence, I will know that you stand firmly in the one Spirit, striving together as one for the faith of the gospel without being frightened in any way by those who oppose you. This is a sign to them that they will be destroyed, but that you will be saved – and that by God. For it has been granted to you on behalf of Christ not only to believe in him, but also to suffer for him."* (Philippians 1:27-29 NIV)

Wait. What? Suffer?

I remember the announcement from The Village Church that Teaching Pastor Matt Chandler had suffered a seizure and was in the hospital. As it turns out, Matt had suffered the seizure due to having a tumor on his brain. It's a long word that I'm not even going to try to spell, but the word meant that the doctors had to act fast and cut out the tumor and some of his frontal lobe. I'm not going to get technical with where the tumor was precisely located, but it was in a bad spot. Matt was given no guarantees that after he awoke from the surgery he would be able to speak. Think about that. Matt, as a communicator of the gospel of Christ, might not be able to talk.

In the subsequent months and years following his surgery Matt endured chemotherapy and other drugs I can't spell, followed by visits to the doctor to monitor his progress. Matt is doing fine today and is the vibrant Teaching Pastor of The Village Church in Flower Mound, Texas. However, the one thing I remember from Matt's sermons following his stay in the hospital and recovery was that he came to the following conclusion: Matt wanted to suffer well.

Wow. *Suffer **well**.*

Why would anyone want to suffer well? Why go through the pain, humiliation, loss, and shame that may come with suffering?

Look folks, I have said before that the Christian life is not sunshine and roses. Jesus said you will suffer and be persecuted for his name's sake. Paul said that people will oppose you for the sake of the gospel, and that you will suffer for Christ.

How do we *suffer well*?

Print this on a poster and hang it in your home. Get it burned into a piece of wood and let it be a decoration in your living room.

> *"Therefore we do not give up. Even though our outer person is being destroyed, our inner person is being renewed day by day. For our **momentary light affliction** is producing for us an absolutely incomparable eternal weight of **glory**. So we do not focus on what is seen, but on what is unseen. For what is seen is temporary, but what is unseen is **eternal**."* (2 Corinthians 2:16-18 HCSB)

A severe sprain is not a barrier to my writing. I may have to use the biblical method of typing (seek and ye shall find) with one finger on one hand, but my mind still works. I can still write and compose. Time off from work provides me with time to minister to others, even in my limited capacity. I can minister to my family. I can still be about the Father's business. I can even stand with Matt Chandler and ask God that I may suffer well in my present situation in life.

Life is going to go wrong, and sometimes horribly so. What will you do in that moment and the moments following? Will you take the advice of Job's wife to "*curse God and die*" (Job 2:9, HCSB) or will you choose to follow the example of Paul who said: "*For me, living is Christ and dying is gain*"? (Philippians 1:21 HCSB)

Once again, this is so important that I must repeat this particular passage. In your particular situation consider the words of Paul to the Philippians. This time from the Holman Christian Standard Bible:

> "*Just one thing: Live your life in a manner* ***worthy*** *of the gospel of Christ. Then, whether I come and see you or am absent, I will hear about you that you are standing firm in one spirit, with one mind, working side by side for the faith that comes from the gospel, not being frightened in any way by your opponents. This is a sign of destruction for them, but of your deliverance – and this is from God. For it has been given to you on Christ's behalf not only to believe in Him, but also to suffer for Him.*" (Philippians 1:27-29 HCSB)

In your hurt, pain, and suffering, pray this with me:

> "*Out of the depths I cry to you, O Lord! O Lord, hear my voice! Let your ears be attentive to the voice of my pleas for mercy! If you, O Lord, should mark iniquities, O Lord, who could stand? But with you there is forgiveness, that you may be feared. I wait for the Lord, my soul waits, and in his word I hope; my soul waits for the Lord more than the watchmen for the morning, more than watchmen for the morning. O Israel, hope in the Lord! For with the Lord there is steadfast love, and with him is plentiful redemption.*

> *And he will redeem Israel from all his iniquities."* (Psalm 130 ESV)

"Lord, hear my cry, hear my plea as I call upon the One who is King eternally. And as I raise my hands I lift my heart, to the risen Lord of all, you are." ("Hear My Cry" by David E. Shelton and Jonathan Mills, © 2009, ASCAP)

If you are suffering and need to know hope, this is my prayer for you:

> *"The Lord bless you and keep you; the Lord make his face shine upon you and be gracious to you; The Lord turn his face toward you and give you peace."* (Numbers 6:24-26 NIV)

EMILY'S AWESOME GOD PRAYER

It's hard to type when you only have one hand. Because I only have one hand to use for typing, I'm grateful for software that helps by typing as I talk. (No, I'm not going to endorse a product here.) In my article *How to Suffer Well* I talked about spraining my wrist. I didn't realize just how good I was at injuring myself. I did a really good job. I did such a good job that I had to have the cyst removed that formed as a result of the accident. I'm hoping that the removal means the end to pain.

During my recovery period I have learned a few things. One of the things I learned is just how much my daughters love me. They brought me drinks, fluffed my pillow, put lotion on my hands that were drying out, and winced with me every time I did something that caused my surgically-repaired right metatarsal appendage to hurt. They also showed me how much they love me because they listen to me. They listen to what I am teaching them about the God I serve.

One of my favorite things to do for my parents is to rewrite popular songs and put words to them that are silly, and reference things that mean something to just us. If I posted the words that talk about chasing squirrels, The St. Louis Cardinals, or QVC it wouldn't mean much. To my parents, the songs are a good opportunity to laugh until they cry. All I can say is, Tim Hawkins, you are in inspiration to me.

Because of that silly song writing I do, my daughters have

aspirations to be silly songwriters...and sometimes serious song writers. My youngest came up to my office last week and was working hard on trying to find the words to put into song. Here is what she came up with:

"Our God is awesome:
Almighty
Wondrous
Everlasting
Son
Of
Man
Elegant and Exalted*

Do you see that? My sixth-grader was making an acrostic from the one word that really only describes God. Okay, I know, that sunset over the white sands of Antigua **is** awesome, but God is more awesome than the sunset He created. I say that He is more awesome because of the words my daughter came up with to describe what "awesome" is in reference to God. Yeah, I know there are not two "e's" on the end of "awesome" but one word there was not enough for her.

My heart sang its own song. I thanked God that my littlest girl believes that these are the words to describe God and who He is: "Almighty, Wondrous, Everlasting, Son of Man, Elegant and Exalted."

What do you think of God? A popular song from the 1960's that found its way into the 1991 Baptist Hymnal asks the question of believing in "more than just a God who didn't care, who lives a way out there?"** Maybe that's your question, too. He's not personal. He's not that awesome. Why do we, the authors and contributors to this website, believe that God is awesome?

A man who did not believe in God once had to acknowledge who God was. This was a king, and not just any king. He was Cyrus, king of Persia, the ruler of most of the world at that time...and he acknowledged who God was after seeing God rescue His servant,

Daniel, from certain death in a den of lions. Have you read these words? Read them again with me:

> *"For He is the living God, enduring forever; His kingdom shall never be destroyed, and His dominion shall be to the end. He delivers and rescues; He works signs and wonders in heaven and on earth, He who has saved Daniel from the power of the lions."* (Daniel 6:26b-27, ESV)

During a tough time just this week, I stood in my office and stared at those words. I have them printed out and hanging on the wall. I look at them every time I want to quit, throw up my hands, and walk away. Every time I was hurting and I couldn't brush my teeth with my right hand. Every time I praised God, something seemed to go wrong...but I looked at those words and praised God still.

Why?

As Chris Tomlin and friends pointed out in song "Whom Shall I Fear":

"I know who goes before me,
I know who stand behind.
The God of angel armies
Is always by my side."***

That is who I want as the object of my worship. A God who really cares. A God who wants to have a relationship with me, and who is more than just a genie who grants my every wish. He gives me what I need...not always what I want...and that makes Him just as awesome, because sometimes what I need is better than what I want.

This is the awesome God, creator of heaven and earth, sustainer of all things, the One who sits enthroned in abject majesty, yet He loves me so much more than I can imagine. He shuts the mouth of lions, he raises the dead, he walks on water, he makes something out of nothing, and he refreshes my life.

Why do we serve Him and implore you, dear reader, to come to a personal relationship with Him? As the Apostle Paul wrote in the fifth chapter of the book Second Corinthians:

> *Therefore, we are ambassadors for Christ, certain that God is appealing through us. We plead on Christ's behalf, "Be reconciled to God." He made the One who did not know sin to be sin for us, so that we might become the righteousness of God in Him."* (2 Corinthians 5:20-21 HCSB)

This "awesome" God, "Almighty, Wondrous, Everlasting, Son of Man, Elegant and Exalted", created the path through Jesus Christ for us to be "reconciled" to him. With all I have written about him in the above words, how could you say no?

Pray with me today to know the one true God, Jehovah… Yahweh…his son, Jesus Christ, and his Spirit that is with us right now:

"Awesome God of heaven and earth, not only do I bend my knee to you today, I bow my heart. I believe in you. I trust you with my life, and I give you my heart and soul. Make me new. Help me to know you as you are…awesome…Almighty, Wondrous, Everlasting, Son of Man, Elegant and Excellent. In the name of your son, Jesus, I pray, amen."

---

*("Our God is Awesome", E.K. Shelton, 2013)

**("He's Everything to Me", Ralph Carmichael, 1964, Communique' Music/ASCAP)

***(Whom Shall I Fear, Chris Tomlin, Ed Cash, Scott Cash, 2012 sixstepsrecords/Sparrow Records)

LIFE HAS CHALLENGES

More than once I have sat holding a phone to my ear in stunned silence unable to believe what I had just heard. I sat through three minutes of accolades only to hear, "We're going with another candidate." I know you, dear reader, can identify with that. Most of us have been through that situation. We've worked hard on knowing the information for the interview, we've rehearsed answers to the impossible questions, and we've asked God in quiet moments for His guidance and favor to get the job we are after.

The jarring aftermath of getting that phone call leads us to one place. Well, it *should* lead us to one place. Everything should lead us to one place - worship.

It is strange that I would think the only place to go after hearing "*we're not picking you*" is before God to worship. It is stranger still when you consider the job that I've been pursuing is that of leading others to worship. What a weird place to be in.

I have had the unenviable task of sitting with a search committee and pouring my heart out about how worship should be a corporate event, but before that it needs to be a personal event borne out of a deep love and devotion to God that causes us to worship. After a week of worship, the culmination is that the Body of Christ gathers to celebrate the week of worship and what God has done to glorify His name. I talk about how the music at the church is not the most important thing I would do, but what **is** important is leading people to worship God in spirit and in truth because of what Christ has done in us. I believe in a Gospel-centered church, and worship that is born out of knowing Christ as Savior. After all of that, I get phrases such as:

> *"Wow, we can't believe you're not already on staff someplace else."*
>
> *"We've never heard it put like that before."*
>
> *"Our committee has never heard of someone with a philosophy of worship. It's very interesting and sounds like what our church needs."*

That's when the feeling washes over me. Words such as those have become a dagger to my heart, because I know what usually follows is a phone call to tell me that the committee is "going in another direction."

Since I was fourteen years old I have believed that God placed a calling on my life to serve in a church as a minister of music leading people in singing of hymns and songs in direct praise of God the Father, Son, and Holy Spirit. I went forward, gave my life to full time Christian service, and even went to seminary.

Thirty-four years later I have only served as part time staff and never full time. "You're a great singer" they say. "We love your voice." Empty, hollow words. I've never had a committee come right out and say that they will not hire someone who has been divorced, but they smile as they walk me to the door and never speak to me again.

This is not a pretty picture I'm painting. I am not sugar-coating the process of becoming employed as a full time staff member of a church.

Your situation may not be that different. Your experience may be in the private sector. Maybe you have been to interview after interview, said all the right things, had all the right credentials, had all the right references, and got what you thought was the wrong phone call or email.

Where does that drive you? Do you run to the bar and over-indulge in alcohol? Or maybe you run to the refrigerator and over-indulge in ice cream. Maybe your heart, in its agony and shame, goes looking for comfort in two-dimensional pictures on the Internet. (Like that's going to help.)

Folks, it drives me to my face before God. I may not literally fall face down on the carpet, but in my heart, I take my devastation and hurt and run hard to God to find out what went so wrong. In my "*wait a minute, what happened*" moment I go to God for the healing balm to soothe my wounded heart. I run to the only thing that will keep the darkness from overwhelming me: worship.

The very thing I want to lead others in doing is what I do when everything has fallen apart. When my plans shatter on the concrete of reality, I sing. I may be in the middle of a broken heart and singing through tears, but the solace that I need is found in worshipping God.

> *"But the hour is coming, and is now here, when the true worshipers will worship the Father in spirit and truth, for the Father is seeking such people to worship him. God is spirit, and those who worship him must worship in spirit and truth."* (John 4:23-24 ESV)

All that I am and all that I have come from God, so even when it is taken from me I still worship the Lord because none of it was mine to begin with. That is a hard place to be, but it is the only place to be.

> *"Worship the Lord in the splendor of holiness; tremble before him, all the earth!" (Psalm 96:9 ESV)*

> *"Ascribe to the Lord the glory due his name; worship the Lord in the splendor of holiness."* (Psalm 29:2 ESV)
>
> *"Exalt the Lord our God, and worship at his holy mountain; for the Lord our God is holy!"* (Psalm 99:9 ESV)
>
> *"Let us go to his dwelling place; let us worship at his footstool!"* (Psalm 132:7 ESV)
>
> *"Oh come, let us worship and bow down; let us kneel before the Lord, our Maker!"* (Psalm 95:6 ESV)

I find no reference in any scripture found in the sixty-six books of the Bible that says, "*When everything is going great, worship God!*" When you don't get the job you think you should have, worship God. When your kids don't obey the first time, when the car gets a flat tire, when the doctor says triplets instead of twins, when the unplanned becomes reality...worship God.

I believe that it is harder to worship God in the good times because we tend to lose focus. Things are going well and worship of God becomes secondary.

I am still working for the same company that I started with almost six years ago. This Sunday morning I will walk into church and step up on the stage to lead worship. I'm not the minister of music. I'm not in charge. I still want to be those things. I still want to be on a church staff, but I will still worship God even though my dream has not come true. I will lead others to worship God. I will sing for an audience of One. I will set aside the things and stuff of earth that has come between me and God, and I will worship Him with abandon.

Why?

The apostle Paul says it best. Grab hold of these words and hang on to them for dear life:

> *"We know that the One who raised the Lord Jesus will raise us also with Jesus and present us with you. Indeed, everything is for your benefit, so that grace, extended through more and more people, may cause thanksgiving to increase to God's glory. Therefore we do not give up. Even though our outer person is being destroyed, our inner person is being renewed day by day.* ***For our momentary light affliction is producing for us an absolutely incomparable eternal weight of glory****. So we do not focus on what is seen, but on what is unseen. For what is seen is temporary, but what is unseen is eternal."* (2 Corinthians 4:14-17 HSCB)

The rough, tough, and rocky road of life takes us through things that would make us want to walk away from God, but we should run to Him and worship. The stuff of earth is "momentary" and does not compare with what is promised to us in that place of perfect peace where Jesus is the source of all light. For this reason alone we should worship God.

Pray with me:

Father, I worship You. I come before You to acknowledge that You alone are worthy to be praised, adored and worshiped. I set aside the things that have come between us. I desire to worship You with abandon, and to worship You in the beauty of Your holiness. Lead me in this path so that I may know you better, and live by the power of Your Spirit. I choose to worship You, even if life is rough, tough, and rocky. You are the God I choose to serve, and the lover of my soul. I worship You, and You alone. For Your beautiful name I pray, amen.

NO SATISFACTION

You may be sitting in your apartment staring at a month's worth of bills that you are not sure how to pay. You may be sitting at your computer in the nook next to the kitchen table where you and your family shared a meal just twenty minutes ago, unable to tell your spouse that you don't want to stay married. You may be sitting at Starbucks over the in the corner next to the window reading this on your mobile device, hoping that no one notices you, but wishing someone would. Wherever you are now reading this article, you have been, or are searching for, "it." What am I talking about? Feeling satisfied.

Admit it, being jazzed about Christmas and the "happy holidays" was what it took to shake off the doldrums of the onset of winter. A couple of Christmas parties and a Christmas program at the local community church helped to ease the downward spiral of life. Now? Well, now it's what another year brings. Nothing that satisfies the longing and emptiness of life.

One-hundred-percent of the people I could survey would complete the following sentence: "All I need to be happy in life is ______________." What would you say? "A new car." "A new pair of shoes." "A new video game (for the gaming generation)." "A visit from my kids." "Being able to visit my kids." How about "more money?" (A possible #1 answer.)

What if you had it all? What if you had more money than anyone else, the biggest elaborate house in the world, more food, more everything? One man did. King Solomon had more of everything than anyone else in the world. His wealth makes Bill Gates look blue collar. His house makes a Beverly Hills mansion look like an efficiency apartment. Here is what he had to say:

> *"All things are wearisome, more than one can say. The eye never has enough of seeing, nor the ear its fill of hearing. What has been will be again, what has been done will be done again;* ***there is nothing new under the sun****. Is there anything of which one can say, "Look! This is something new"? It was here already, long ago; it was here before our time."* (Ecclesiastes 1:8-10 NIV84, emphasis mine)

> *"I have seen all the things that are done under the sun; all of them are meaningless, a chasing after the wind."* (Ecclesiastes 1:14 NIV84)

What are you chasing that is meaningless? There is nothing, nor no one who will bring you the satisfaction that you are longing to latch onto in hopes of dispelling the emptiness of your life.

So why pray to God?

In a recent conversation someone implied that many forms of religion have the same goals. This was after I had pointed out that Christianity was different because of the change God makes in our lives. My counterpart argued that the same results could come from any religion. I disagreed and here's why: The Bible says that if we are led by the Spirit of God this is what our lives will look like:

> *"But the fruit of the Spirit is love, joy, peace, patience, kindness, goodness, faithfulness, gentleness, self-control; against such things there is no law."* (Ephesians 5:22-23 ESV)

Did you see that? Let's back up so you don't miss it. "*But the fruit of the Spirit...*" Now do you see it?

Here is the difference between the relationship with God found in Christianity and every other religion in the world: You can't do it. Because of the relationship you have with the sovereign God of this universe, what can flow out of your life by ***His*** Spirit is love, joy, peace, patience, kindness, goodness, faithfulness, gentleness, and self-control. It is the Spirit of God living in you. You can't do this on your own.

No other religion makes this claim. All of the other religions of this world say that you can accomplish it all on your own - and you and I both know that's a complete lie. If it were true, you wouldn't be reading this article because I wouldn't be writing it because of my experiences, and there would be no need for the self-help books found in every bookstore across the United States. You and I would have no need of praying to Jehovah God.

Love. Joy. Peace. Patience. Kindness. Goodness. Faithfulness. Gentleness. Self-Control.

Examine those words for a moment. Look at each one and spend a moment to dwell on the meaning of that word. Would your life, would my life have much more meaning if all of these things flowed out of us as a result of our relationship with Jesus Christ? Absolutely!

We expend so much energy working towards the stuff of earth that cannot satisfy that we spend little time with God. Our lives have things like envy, anger, jealousy, sadness, impatience, and greed flowing out of us. This is the result of us attempting to do things on our own.

Right here, right now, pray with me...not just on your own, but *with* me to ask God for His Spirit to be poured out in our lives that people may see the fruit that comes from a relationship with Him.

"Father God, I'm sorry for attempting to fill up my life with the "stuff of earth". Forgive me for trying to replace your good gifts with things that only satisfy for a moment. I ask for your Spirit to dwell in

every area of my life so that what flows out of me is the evidence of your grace. Help me to be the example of your mercy as love, joy, peace, patience, kindness, goodness, faithfulness, gentleness, and self-control flow from me to others because of the work of Your Spirit in my life. Help me to walk out of the darkness I have allowed into my life and walk into Your everlasting, marvelous light. In the name of your son, Jesus, I pray. Amen."

I leave you with these words of comfort:

> *"And this is his commandment, that we believe in the name of his Son Jesus Christ and love one another, just as he has commanded us. Whoever keeps his commandments abides in God, and God in him. And by this we know that he abides in us, by the Spirit whom he has given us."* (1 John 3:23-24 HCSB)

PRECIOUS MEMORIES

I grew up singing in small churches all over the state of Illinois. We sang a lot of the old Gospel songs and hymns from years past. One song that my dad would sing was "Precious Memories." The chorus says, "Precious memories, how they linger, how they ever flood my soul. In the stillness of the midnight, precious, sacred scenes unfold." Why "precious memories?" I ask, why not? The Apostle Paul says think on the good things:

> *"Finally brothers, whatever is true, whatever is honorable, whatever is just, whatever is pure, whatever is lovely, whatever is commendable – if there is any moral excellence and if there is any praise – dwell on these things."* (Philippians 4:8 HCSB)

What brought this to mind was something my dad wrote to me in an e-mail. My dad will send me random e-mails, but I have kept every single one because they are written in his unique way. The stories he recounts are precious to me because they are mostly good memories. I want to keep them as long as I can. One in particular stood out. Here is an excerpt:

"I am sitting here with a small afghan (Mother called it a "lapaghan") made several years ago. There are 12 strips, 4 inches wide, crocheted together to make this "lapaghan." She originally made them with the idea they could be sold, but they were never sold. Instead, she

gave them away as gifts and donated one to be raffled at the annual Alumni banquet as a fund raiser.

Mother was always involved in crafts. For years she went to her church every Thursday to quilt with other women. She was a member of the Home Bureau and they were always making something, crafty. She made clothes such as shirts and dresses. She quilted, crocheted, tatted, and fixed her boys' jeans that needed new knee patches.

As I sit here and think about her talents I am amazed. She spent her last 8 years at the nursing home. Along the way someone gave her a hot pad holder made from plastic beads. She saw a flaw in the pattern, so she had me get the supplies she needed and she began to make beaded pot holders without the flaw. Again, they were given as gifts. The cost of the beads was minimal, but consumed many hours of her time; but each project had to be done just right.

Later as her fingers stiffened and her concentration was not good she tried to make another lapaghan. The results were not good and she asked me to find someone to finish her work.

Looking back as I sit here, warmed by the lapaghan Mother made, I am reminded of the thought and dedication that went into the making of it. I think back fondly and it brings back many memories of home and family. Mother has been gone nearly four years and the love she put into the lapaghan is still warming me."

Precious memories. A connection to the past. Warm thoughts, that wrap you in an embrace that is timeless and reminds us that we are not forgotten or alone. We are loved. God's love is the same.

> *"For this reason, I kneel before the Father of our Lord Jesus Christ, from whom every family in heaven and on earth is named. I pray that He may grant you, according to the riches of His glory, to be strengthened with power in the inner man through His Spirit, and that the Messiah may dwell in your hearts through faith. I pray that you, being rooted and firmly established in love, may be able to comprehend with*

> *all the saints what is the length and width, height and depth of God's love, and to know the Messiah's love that surpasses knowledge, so you may be filled with all the fullness of God."* (Ephesians 3:14-19 HCSB)

God wants to wrap you in a warm embrace. You won't be able to comprehend how far God's arms go around you, above you, behind you, beside you, above you, below you or in any direction you want to measure. He wants to be more than the "lapaghan." He wants to cover you completely.

He calls us his children, because as a good father he wraps us up in arms of love. Not necessarily to protect us, but to give us the inner strength to:

- get out of bed one more time
- do that homework project for one more hour
- do those extra sit-ups
- run that extra mile
- go back to the loathsome job
- drive to one more practice/rehearsal
- pack one more lunch

Dear reader, God is not enabling you to sit and cower in fear. He is giving you the power to stand up and do something! The Apostle Paul's prayer to the Ephesian church was for power:

> *"I pray that He may grant you, according to the riches of His glory, to be strengthened with power in the inner man through His Spirit,"* (Ephesians 3:16 HCSB)

Mourn through the dark night of the soul! Cry out to God in desperation! Kneel before Him and beg forgiveness for your sins! Cry with the broken-hearted! Sit in sackcloth and ashes…just don't stay there! Paul says to stand up! Put on your armor and take a stand:

> *"This is why you must take up the full armor of God, so that you may be able to resist evil in that day, and having prepared everything, to take your stand."* (Ephesians 6:13 HCSB)

I look at my grandmother's handiwork every day. It's in the form of a quilt that covers my bed. Every stitch in it was done by her hands. Yes, the quilt keeps me warm on cold nights, but it is her enduring love that has prompted me many times to keep going. Her abiding love of Christ through her 90-plus years lovingly pushed me to be nearer to Him.

We see God's handiwork everywhere. Louie Giglio's presentation titled "Indescribable" shows us God's immense power and handiwork in the universe through Hubble telescope and Voyager Space probe images. We're a blue speck in a bright beam of sunlight against the vastness of the Milky Way. We're on the edge of the galaxy that is very small compared to the rest of the universe. He knows every star by name. He measures the universe with the span of his hand. The morning stars sing together to proclaim his majesty in the heavens.

Yet, he cares for us. For you and for me. Hold on to your precious memories. May they linger and encourage you in the dark of the night. However, may the love of God in Christ Jesus empower you to stand.

Pray with me: *"Father, sometimes it is very hard to feel you near me. It's hard to know you love me when my world is crashing down all around me. My heart and mind fight over whether you are real or not. I ask that your love would surround me and drive away the darkness in my soul and in my life. I need your light to shine through the darkness to my soul and fill me with your presence and your power. Help me to stand up and keep going. I'm asking you for this power because I have none on my own. The Bible says "the heavens declare the glory of God". Please declare your glory in and through me. I need you so much and I cannot make it without you. In the name of your son, Jesus, I pray, amen."*

DEATH IS NOT THE END

Moments in time can take your breath away. In "*The Lord of the Rings: Return of the King*" Gandalf called it the "deep breath before the hammer stroke." I had such a moment on Wednesday, August 17, 2016. At 4pm that afternoon I sat down to my computer to do some work and opened the app on my phone to Facebook to check for updates while my computer booted up. The first story on my feed took my breath away.

Preston Harris, a friend from my days at Wedgwood Baptist Church in Fort Worth, stepped from this life into the next as his earthen vessel, his jar of clay lost the fight with cancer. Preston was only forty-years old. Preston left behind a wife, Julie, and two teenage daughters close to the age of my own daughters. Many thoughts and emotions flooded my heart and soul as the news soaked in. I sang a lot of music with this guy on several occasions, and did life with him and his family for several years.

I knew Preston had been ill, as I had followed his journey on social media for the past year. I really thought that he would be one of those who would beat the killer disease. Not this time.

My mind raced to what Julie must be going through with a long-fought struggle finally being over, but at the same time, she lost the love of her life. Preston and Julie's daughters lost their dad. He won't be walking them down the aisle. He won't be bouncing grandkids on his knee and teaching them the songs of worship that tell of the Savior he loved so much. Preston won't be there to help Julie figure out what's next. He won't be there to help her figure out how to pay for college, buy new cars, repair the toilet that's not flushing, change air filters in the AC system, bring in firewood for the fireplace in the winter, nor will he be there to lead his family.

The hammer fell at 2:05pm Wednesday. Preston breathed his last.

In this world.

> *"Brothers and sisters, we do not want you to be uninformed about those who sleep in death, so that you do not grieve like the rest of mankind, who have no hope."* (1 Thessalonians 4:13 NIV)

> *"Precious in the sight of the Lord is the death of His faithful servants."* (Psalm 116:15 NIV)

> *"For we know that if the earthly tent we live in is destroyed, we have a building from God, an eternal house in heaven, not built by human hands. Meanwhile we groan, longing to be clothed instead with our heavenly dwelling, because when we are clothed, we will not be found naked. For while we are in this tent, we groan and are burdened, because we do not wish to be unclothed but clothed instead with our heavenly dwelling, so that what is mortal may be swallowed up by life."* (2 Corinthians 5:1-4 NIV)

> *"Now there is in store for me the crown of righteousness, which the Lord, the righteous Judge, will award to me on that day – and not only to me, but also to all who have longed for his appearing."* (2 Timothy 4:8 NIV)

> *"Where, O death, is your victory? Where, O death, is your sting?"* (1 Corinthians 15:55 NIV)

> *"I assure you: If anyone keeps My word, he will never see death – ever!"* (John 8:51 HCSB)

I firmly believe that while Preston's older brother led the family in worship around the hospital bed in that house, Jesus had stepped into the room. He was there when Death showed up.

Why was Jesus there?

> *"Don't be afraid! I am the First and the Last, and the Living One. I was dead, but look – I am alive forever and ever, and I hold the keys to death and Hades."* (Revelation 1:17b-18 HCSB)

Death came calling for Preston's body, but Jesus had charge of the situation. Since Jesus was in charge of the situation Death took the breath from Preston's body, but Jesus took his soul.

I know. I hear you. You're asking how can anyone know for certain? How can anyone know that Jesus is there in that moment of death and that John 8:51 (referenced above) is true?

Jesus said so.

Go with me to Calvary. Let's walk in the past and stand at the foot of three crosses on the hill called "The place of the skull." We see three people crucified; two are recognizable thieves from Jerusalem. Everyone knows that they have a bad reputation and that they are getting what they deserve. One of the two thieves crucified on one side of Jesus hurled insults at Jesus. He tells Jesus to save himself and them! The other thief speaks because he recognizes the situation and who is in it:

> *"But the other answered, rebuking him: 'Don't you even fear God, since you are undergoing the same punishment? We are punished justly, because we're getting back what we deserve for the things we did, but this man has done nothing wrong.' Then he said, 'Jesus, remember me when*

> *you come into your kingdom!' And He said to him, 'I assure you:* ***Today*** *you will be with me in paradise."* (Luke 23:40-43 HCSB, emphasis mine)

> *'I assure you:* ***Today*** *you will be with me in paradise.*

Did you see that? The answer was "today". At the point of death the thief on the cross would go **with** Jesus to paradise. He holds the keys. He's in charge. Death did not win then and it will not win now.

Preston met death on that Wednesday, but he was not alone. Jesus was there, holding the keys and the promise to the thief was the same for Preston: Paradise. Death probably had to bow to the King. He probably called out Preston's name. The body quit, but the soul stepped out and Jesus took Preston by the hand and they went to Paradise.

> "*Yes, we are of good courage and we would rather be away from the body and at home with the Lord.*" (2 Corinthians 5:8 ESV)

Courage.
Paradise.
Today.
Blessed assurance.
Jesus.

Folks, this is how Christians like Preston and Julie prepare for and handle death. This is how Julie got out of bed today and will continue to do so until she too leaves this world. The knowledge of the presence of God in all things, including death, is the hope that we have which the world does not understand. This is what we know. Life doesn't end at the death of the body; it changes gears.

When Christians die, he or she becomes more powerful than you can image. We are given a new body that is impervious to death, sickness, disease (cancer) and decay. We are changed to be like Christ, and He is Lord of All, Creator of the universe, and death has no power over him. As humans we see the power of life and death as the greatest power in the world. Jesus has power over both.

We will be like Him, so that makes us very powerful after we leave this world. Death will have no power over us and we will bow only at the feet of Jesus and worship at His throne.

We as Christians have hope. HOPE! Who is our hope? Jesus, the Christ, the Son of the Living God. He is in charge and will make us and this world what it was originally intended to be.

Behold, I am making
all things new.'

"And he who was seated on the throne said, 'Behold, I am making all things new.' Also, he said, 'Write this down, for these words are trustworthy and true."
(Revelation 21:5 ESV)

'Write this down,
for these words are
trustworthy and true.

Do you need hope? Do you need assurance that death is not the end? Ask Jesus for the assurance of a hope that you cannot see and the faith to believe:

"Jesus, right now I need you. I need you to be in this moment and every moment from here until I draw my last breath. I give you my life

and I turn away from what has kept us apart; all of the things that you count as sin, I walk away from them and turn to you. Give me the faith to believe, give me your assurance, change my heart, wash it clean and make me whiter than snow on the inside. Help me to know for certain that when death calls for me You will be there to take me to Paradise to be with You forever. In your name I pray, amen."

"I will rise when He calls my name
No more sorrow, no more pain
I will rise on eagles wings
Before my God fall on my knees and rise
*I will rise."**

---

*("I will Rise" Lyrics Copyright © Chris Tomlin, Jesse Reeves, Louie Giglio, Matt Maher, Passion and ThankYou Music)

ONE STEP AT A TIME

I can say with all sincerity that I have few actual heroes. There are just a handful of men who have had a profound impact on my life. Many have spoken into my life, but only a few have made a lasting impression. One of those men is Don Owens. I list Don as one of my heroes because he lives his life like I want to live mine: filled with adventure. Of the men I have met over my forty-nine years, Don is the one who has embodied "Wild At Heart."

Don has been around the world and had adventures that most guys only dream about. He has run with the bulls in Pamplona, soaked in the hot springs of Iceland, and became a member of the "14-er's" club. Yeah, I didn't know what that meant either until I read what Don wrote about it on a social media site.

People who do "14-er's" are those adventuresome individuals who hike up mountain peaks that are at least fourteen-thousand feet in elevation. The first time I read about Don's adventure up a fourteen-thousand-foot peak, I thought he was crazy. Why would anyone do that? Now I know why: for the adventure.

The other question that really kept me pondering was "How do you do that?" How do you get up the mountain and get that high up? I figured it out.

In April of 2015 I had my gallbladder removed. My diseased gall bladder had me believing I was having heart attacks. I thought I was so out of shape that I would never be able to do anything physical ever again. A year after my gallbladder removal surgery my wife and

I hiked up the side of a mountain in Colorado; the elevation was roughly six-thousand feet. At the beginning of July of 2016 we went to Mammoth Cave National Park in Kentucky for a family vacation stop. We set out on a trail through the park to enjoy the wonderful evening weather and see all the creation God had placed in the park. I was now able to hike long distances after conquering Helen Hunt Falls in Colorado Springs.

As I started out on the trail I wound up in the back of our family carrying the backpack laden with snacks and drinks. I watched my wife and kids go on ahead and start to point out things on the trail. God pointed something out to me.

As a percussionist down to my very core, my life involves a lot of rhythm. Walking is a rhythm for me. I walk to a beat or a metronome in my head. My pace varies with where I am going or what the task is. If on an evening walk with my wife, it's a little more fast-paced to burn more calories. If strolling through the mall or down the main street of Targu Mures, Romania, my pace is slower to enjoy the surroundings and take in the scenery. I discovered about myself that on a trail I tend to set an even pace; not too fast, not too slow. They are measured, even steps so that I don't go too fast or too slow, but at a pace that will get me to my desired destination at the end of the trail, or up the side of the mountain without blowing through all my energy. *One step at a time.* There it was! Walking along this serene trail I uncovered Don's secret to making it up to fourteen-thousand feet: *one step at a time.*

My friend, dear reader, beloved by God, this is how we make it through life. One step at a time walking with God.

> "*The Lord makes firm the steps of the one who delights in him.*" (Psalm 37:23 NIV)

> "*I have considered my ways and have turned my steps to your statutes.*" (Psalm 119:59 NIV)

> *"Righteousness goes before him and prepares the ways for his steps."* (Psalm 85:13 NIV)

Whether climbing the mountain or walking along the marked path through a forest, we get to the top of the mountain or the end of the trail one step at a time.

The Apostle Paul wrote in his letter to the Corinthians:

> *"Do you not know that in a race all the runners run, but only one gets the prize? Run in such a way as to get the prize."* (1 Corinthians 9:24 NIV)

The concept is the same. To win a race, you must successfully put one foot in front of the other, and the fastest runner does not always win. The runner who paces himself throughout the race will win.

One step at a time.

I'm not in the same physical shape as Don. I can't go out this weekend and follow Don up the side of a fourteen-thousand-foot mountain and summit the peak. I can prepare, get in shape, and follow him up to the summit one step at a time.

Are some steps harder than others? Yes. We sometimes run out of strength.

> *"But those who hope in the Lord will renew their strength. They will soar on wings like eagles, they will run and not be weary, they will walk and not be faint."* (Isaiah 40:31 NIV)

Don't give up. Don't give in. Take one more step and then another and then another. Keep going. Your Father will be with you every step of the way.

"Father, I come to you now asking that you give me the strength for one more step, and one more after that, and one more after that. Keep me connected to you by your Spirit because you are the vine that gives us life, and everything we need comes from you. Whether I am climbing a mountain, walking along a trail, or pushing through one of the storms of life guide my steps. Let "your word be a lamp for my feet and a light on my path" (Psalm 119:105 NIV) so that I can follow you all the days of my life. In the name of your risen Son, Jesus, amen.

FINDING INNER PEACE

I found myself standing alone, the wind blowing over me from left to right. Every eight to ten seconds there was a crash that was deafening. With every crash my feet sank. Sounds like a very bad situation, one where you, the reader, are waiting for ka-boom! or a gun shot or crash of a car.

This moment in time was not a bad situation; it was a moment of worship.

I found myself standing alone on the beach staring out into the vast water that made up the Gulf of Mexico as far as I could see. The winds off of the oceanic waters blew through my hair from left to right as I faced the vast expanse of salt water. Every eight to ten seconds there was a crash of waves that was deafening as the waves roared their multitudinous voices back to the Maker who set their boundaries. With every crash of the waves my feet sank in the sand as the water washed over me.

Every time I stand on the edge of the water I am reminded that Creator God, Father of all, Master of this universe holds all of this together. God knows the exact number of grains of sand. He knows the exact number of flotsam and jetsam that litters the beach. God instructed the waters of the ocean to come to this gulf coast and go no further.

> *Who enclosed the sea behind doors when it burst from the womb, when I made the clouds its garment and*

> *thick darkness its blanket, when I determined its boundaries and put [its] bars and doors in place, when I declared: "You may come this far, but no farther; your proud waves stop here."?* (Job 38:8-11 HCSB)

As I stood on the beach, the stuff of earth melted away. Instead of asking for peace I was thanking God for peace.

I agree it's crazy to have to drive to the edge of the North American gulf coast to find peace, but sometimes we must get away from the trees to be able to see the forest. Sometimes we must get far enough back from the trouble that finds us every day to be able to see God's goodness, mercy, and grace.

That may be a country road far enough out from the city so that you can see more stars in the night sky. Maybe your spot is on the fourteenth row of the bleachers at the practice field. From "your spot" you love to watch the sun set as brilliant pink and orange colors fill the sky. Maybe your time to get away from the trees is that morning run where you purposefully run towards the east so that you can see the sun rise and greet the new day.

I can still feel the cool gulf waters as they wash over my feet. I can smell the salty air. I hear the crash of the waves and the cries of the sea gulls. Find your place and pray with me:

> *"Father, I know you have created everything. I thank you for this moment of peace and reminding me of how deep Your love is for me. Help me to hear Your voice today. Thank You for Your peace that passes all understanding."*

> *"May the Lord of peace Himself give you peace always in every way. The Lord be with all of you."* (2 Thessalonians 3:16 HCSB)

THE JOB MOMENT

I sat listening as my friend, Karl, told me about a moment in his life that I call the "Job moment," after the man in the Bible named Job who was severely tested when he lost everything. Here's what my friend Karl described as his "Job moment".

Karl sat back in the chair dumbfounded. His mind raced to process what had heard. The pastor sat across the desk staring at Karl and was waiting for a response. The pastor had just asked Karl to sign the contract, resign the following Sunday, and speak to no one about what had just happened in that room. Karl was to tell no one of the contract that forced him to be silent so that Karl could receive a severance package over the next two months. The contract also forced him and his family to move out of the parsonage. If there was any damage to the home deemed unreasonable, the cost to repair the damage would be deducted from the final paycheck.

Karl sat there lost for just a moment reflecting on the past six months. Hospitalized for a week in January due to a pinhole perforation in his lower intestine, he came home to the pastor telling Karl that his job performance was poor. Karl was the minister of music, administration and children for the small church that averaged one-hundred-fifty in attendance. Karl had also been given the task of overseeing Vacation Bible School and taking the children to camp. It was not long after this poor job review that Karl came down with a severe case of bronchitis. His voice was not strong enough, but anyone who has battled the illness knows that your voice suffers when there is fluid in the lungs. All the coughing irritates the vocal chords.

Now, his ministry and job were being taken away by a group of people in the church, of all places, who did not want the rest of the congregation to know what was happening.

Karl was in his "Job moment."

Have you had a "Job moment?" That moment when everything you have is taken away? That moment when everything goes completely sideways and out of control, and all you can do is sit and watch. Here's the original "Job moment" to help you, dear reader, identify:

> *"There was a man in the land of Uz whose name was Job, and that man was blameless and upright, one who feared God and turned away from evil. There were born to him seven sons and three daughters. He possessed 7,000 sheep, 3,000 camels, 500 yoke of oxen, and 500 female donkeys, and very many servants, so that this man was the greatest of all the people of the east."* (Job 1:1-3 ESV)
>
> *"Now there was a day when the sons of God came to present themselves before the LORD, and Satan also came among them. The LORD said to Satan, "From where have you come?" Satan answered the LORD and said, "From going to and fro on the earth, and from walking up and down on it." And the LORD said to Satan, "Have you considered my servant Job, that there is none like him on the earth, a blameless and upright man, who fears God and turns away from evil?" Then Satan answered the LORD and said, "Does Job fear God for no reason? Have you not put a hedge around him and his house and all that he has, on every side? You have blessed the work of his hands, and*

> *his possessions have increased in the land. But stretch out your hand and touch all that he has, and he will curse you to your face." And the LORD said to Satan, "Behold, all that he has is in your hand. Only against him do not stretch out your hand." So Satan went out from the presence of the LORD."* (Job 1:6-12)

> *The oxen were plowing and the donkeys feeding beside them, and the Sabeans fell upon them and took them and struck down the servants with the edge of the sword, and I alone have escaped to tell you." While he was yet speaking, there came another and said, "The fire of God fell from heaven and burned up the sheep and the servants and consumed them, and I alone have escaped to tell you." While he was yet speaking, there came another and said, "The Chaldeans formed three groups and made a raid on the camels and took them and struck down the servants with the edge of the sword, and I alone have escaped to tell you." While he was yet speaking, there came another and said, "Your sons and daughters were eating and drinking wine in their oldest brother's house, and behold, a great wind came across the wilderness and struck the four corners of the house, and it fell upon the young people, and they are dead, and I alone have escaped to tell you."* (Job 1:14-19 ESV)

This is the "Job moment". Everything is gone. What do you do? It doesn't have to be a minister losing his job; it could be you losing your family, your home, your career, and all of it in an instant. The important question to ask here is not "Why," but "What." *What* will you do? Do you shake your fist to heaven and blame God for every bad thing that happened or do you respond like Job did.

> *"Then Job arose and tore his robe and shaved his head and fell on the ground and worshiped. And he said, "Naked I came from my mother's womb, and naked shall I return. The LORD gave, and the LORD has taken away; blessed be the name of the LORD." In all this Job did not sin or charge God with wrong."* (Job 1:20-22 ESV)

I sat with my friend, Karl, and asked him the very same question. I reminded him of Job and how this was his "Job moment." The choice to reject God and the church he has faithfully served for over twenty years or run toward God and let Him be God. I encourage him every week to run towards God and lead his family to worship God.

- God did not let Karl down.
- God did not fire Karl.
- God did not draw up the secret contract.
- God did not force Karl and his family to vacate the parsonage. These things were done by fallen, sinful men.

I too have suffered from hurtful situations. In those situations I have looked around and found that Job's response is the only response. I have had to say in some very tough times that God "gives and takes away," especially when I don't understand.

Are you in this moment right now? Are you looking around to see where everyone has run off to?

> *The name of the Lord is a strong tower; the righteous man runs into it and is safe.* (Proverbs 18:10 ESV)

> *Hear my cry, O God, listen to my prayer; from the end of the earth I call to you when my heart is faint. Lead me to the rock that is higher than I, for you have been*

> *my refuge, a strong tower against the enemy. Let me dwell in your tent forever! Let me take refuge under the shelter of your wings!* (Psalm 61:1-4 ESV)

"Father, we cry out to you. We have no other one in all of the world who will love us as you do, and care for us as you do...even when we are hurting as bad as we are hurting right now. Be near. Show us your presence and your glory. Show us that it is not you who is intent on causing us pain or hurt. Please give us your peace that is only found in you. You alone are good. You alone are worthy. You alone are God. You alone love us as none other will ever love us. Hear our cry, O God, and listen to our prayer. In the name of your son, Jesus, whose life, death and resurrection made this relationship possible, amen.

Karl's name was changed to protect him and his family.

TRUST IN THE LORD

> *"Trust in the Lord with all your heart, and do not rely on your own understanding; think about Him in all your ways, and He will guide you on the right paths. Don't consider yourself to be wise; fear the Lord and turn away from evil. This will be healing for your body and strengthening for your bones."* (Proverbs 3:5-8 HCSB)

As I sat in the faux leather chair behind my desk in my office I felt very small. The words that were just spoken from the other side of the desk had pierced my heart like a spear. That moment will be frozen in time for me. My friend sat across from me with tears in his eyes. The words from his mouth were directed by the Spirit of God and hung in the air: *"Do you trust God?"*

My mind raced, "Of course, I trust God…I think. I'm supposed to, I mean, I'm a Christian and Christians trust God. Don't they? That comes with being a Christian, right?"

I had just unloaded everything that had been bottled up inside me and I wanted someone to listen. I felt let down by my friends and felt an undue burden because of "those people" who didn't come through when I needed them. My problems were mounting. I needed someone to care. Where were these people when I needed them most? Where was my family? Why didn't one of my family members step up to the plate and help correct the situation?

As a small business owner I don't have a manager or supervisor to report to. I own the business, but I do represent a larger company. It's akin to being a franchise owner. If I had a supervisor or manager, it would be Omarr. Some people wonder why they get placed in certain places. I know the hand of Providence placed me in my business so that Omarr and I could become friends, and later find out we are brothers in Christ. The company I represent is filled with people who are Christians and live it out loud. Omarr is among them.

As we sat in my office, after I had unloaded and lamented why life was not being fair, the meeting about numbers and goals turned into a prayer meeting as I finally told Omarr what was on my heart. The one thing I wanted: rest. I wanted rest from my troubles, trials, and labors of this world, but I know that I haven't been called Home. I wanted to lean against my Father's chest and listen to His heartbeat, close my eyes as that rhythm fills my hearing, and rest. We stopped, Omarr prayed, and the healing began.

Is this you? The war of Life is raging, sometimes violently. Day after day you fight on, but all you want is to rest. You're tired of the fight. You're tired of having to battle it out from the time you wake up, and then the battle does not cease, even when you finally drift off to sleep in exhaustion. That was me. *Was* me.

The following Sunday our pastor read the words of Proverbs 3:5 and I continued to verse eight. They are important enough for me to write again:

> "*Trust in the Lord with all your heart, and do not rely on your own understanding; think about Him in all your ways, and He will guide you on the right paths. Don't consider yourself to be wise; fear the Lord and turn away from evil. This will be healing for your body and strengthening for your bones.*" (Proverbs 3:5-8 HCSB)

Did you see it? Look back at where I had placed my trust. I was relying on man instead of God. People let me down. Why was I shocked? We've been letting each other down for centuries and it was a surprise to me!

"Trust in the Lord with all your heart..."

Focus. I lacked focus.

Misplaced trust. I trusted in men.

I was not close to God. I felt far from Him.

In 1982, the St. Louis Cardinals were the best team in baseball and proved it by winning the World Series. I followed them closely because I wanted to play for them. I wanted to play second base next to Ozzie Smith, the "Wizard of Ahhs," at shortstop. Tommy Herr was the Cardinals second baseman at the time. I envied him. My lasting image of Tommy Herr, a switch-hitting player who was good enough to go to the All-Star game in 1985, was of him standing at second base with one foot on the bag looking down, hands on his hips, a bit of dejection on his face because there were now three outs. Alone on second base; Tommy had done his part, but it wasn't enough. Second base is very far from the dugout when the inning is over and you have to jog back in. In reality, it's not that far, but it seems a long ways away when things haven't gone right.

That was me in life. I felt as though I was alone on second, but dejected because it wasn't enough. I had done my part, but it didn't change the outcome and my team let me down. That, my friends, is **not** the Christian life. That is not what Christ has called us to.

If you're searching for the answers to life, if you feel as though your Christian walk looks like a dejected runner at second base with no outs left, if you can't understand why you pray and nothing ever changes, maybe it's because you are not focused on the One in whom to place your trust.

The new book "Moving Mountains" by John Eldridge* (author of "Wild At Heart" and "Fathered by God") is a transformative book on prayer that changed my prayer life forever. One paragraph from that book shows us that prayer is not what we have thought it to be:

> *"We know who he is and who we are. We know what is going on in the world. We understand the invasion, and that we are partners with God invoking the kingdom. We know prayer is not begging God, nor is it merely a zap. So, let us kill this religious deception with an axe and bury it forever. It was not given to us by Jesus."***

To understand this paragraph requires ninety-five pages of reading or a summation like this: What prayer has been for most of us is not what God ever intended it to be. We are not outsiders to the Kingdom of God. Those of us called by His name have been *invited* into the throne room of God. We have been asked to be a part of the inner circle:

> *"I do not call you slaves anymore, because a slave doesn't know what his master is doing. I have called you friends, because I have made known to you everything I have heard from My Father."* (John 15:15 HCSB)

"Invasion," "partners," "invoking," "not begging" - words not usually associated with prayer.

Do you cry out to God as if he is so far away that you must shout, hoping to be heard? The Psalmist said that God is *"near to the broken-hearted."* (Psalm 34:18) When we pray we should be bold, as sons of the King, and in our hearts walk into the throne room of our Father and talk with him as his children and heirs:

> *"Let us then approach God's throne of grace with confidence, so that we may receive mercy and find grace to help us in our time of need."* (Hebrews 4:16, NIV)

My issue with trusting God has been put to rest and the God of all grace and mercy has begun repairing my wounded heart. I now go to God, not as some other-worldly being seated on a throne of majesty in a nebula somewhere way in the outer reaches of the universe, but as the Father of my heart who is eager to listen. He is waiting to hear me. He wants me to get to know Him better and understand how we are going to work together in any given situation.

My children have never asked if they could come to the table when a meal is served. I make a place for them. I put out a knife, fork and spoon, a plate for their food, a cup for their drink (unless they insist on drinking from a can) and enough food for them to eat and be satisfied. Why would the God of this universe, whom we call "Father," do anything less for his children? Wrap your mind around that thought and your approach to prayer will change. Learn to trust in God with all of your heart and allow him to direct your path in life. He will lead you places you never dreamed of going. He will also answer prayer in ways you never expected. Become that heir to the kingdom. Be who God called you to be: His.

Pray with me:

Father God, you have made everything I see, and you hold it all together. You sit enthroned in majesty in the heavens, but you rule my heart from within. I give up. I give you everything. I let go of the things on this earth that I have made more important than you. I place my trust in you and remove it from men. Men will fail me. You will never fail. Give us today all that we need, and forgive us because we have failed you. Help us to forgive those who have failed us. Show us how to trust in you and lead us on your path of righteousness. Keep the evil one far from us and remove his work so that your kingdom may grow. You are the only God, Most High. We praise you and thank you. In the name of your son, Jesus, the Risen One, we pray. Amen.

SOMEONE TO LOVE ME

I don't know of a single person who has **never** wanted to be loved. I can't think of anyone that I know who does not want to be loved. Everyone wants to be loved by someone else. Everyone wants to feel special to someone. Children want their parent's affection; husbands long for their wives to love them deeply; wives long for their husbands to love them deeply.

I recently sat in the *Life Today* studio and listened to James Robison teach about God's love for us. James talked about how God wants to love us like a father loves his children, and he pointed us to a verse that I did not know was in the Bible. It was one of those that I had possibly read before, but it did not jump out at me like it did at that moment. Read this passage from John 17:

> *"My prayer is not for them (the Disciples) alone. I pray also for those who will believe in me through their message, that all of them may be one, Father, just as you are in me and I am in you. May they also be in us so that the world may believe that you have sent me. I have given them the glory that you gave me, that they may be one as we are one— I in them and you in me—so that they may be brought to complete unity. Then the world will know that you sent me and have* ***loved them even as you have loved me.***" (John 17:20-23 NIV, emphasis mine)

Do you see the depth of the Father's love? Right there in the last sentence: "*Then the world will know that you sent me* ***and have loved them even as you have loved me.***" In this sentence Jesus makes the statement that God loves us as much as he loves Jesus. It's a declarative statement. Jesus isn't asking God to love us in this prayer. He's not begging. This definitive statement says God has loved all of us *"even as you have loved me (Jesus)."*

Take just a moment to let that sink in. Jesus has just made this statement: God loves us as much as he loves Jesus. Here it is one more time: God loves **us** *as much as* he loves Jesus.

The apostle Paul put it this way in his letter to the Ephesian church:

> *I pray that you, being rooted and firmly established in love, may be able to comprehend with all the saints what is the* ***length and width, height and depth of God's love****, and to know the Messiah's love that surpasses knowledge, so you may be filled with all the fullness of God.* (Ephesians 3:17b-19 HCSB)

How deep is God's love? Dive down and try to find the bottom. You'll never reach the bottom of God's love.

How wide is God's love? Try going around it. You'll never find a corner to turn at the end of God's love.

How high is God's love? If your rocket-boosted space capsule went straight up after exiting earth's atmosphere with the proper trajectory, you could never get high enough to get over the top of God's love.

I have been wrestling with the vastness of God's love ever since that day. I have been trying to wrap my brain around what all of this means to me. I have been attempting to reconcile my heart to the magnitude of the love of God for someone like me. Here is what I've been able to come up with:

Even in my brokenness, God loves me.
Even in my pain, God loves me.
Even in my sin, God loves me.
Even in my suffering, God loves me.
Even in my crushed spirit, God loves me.
Even when I don't follow him, God loves me.
Even when I don't trust him, God loves me.
Even when I am in deep despair, God loves me.
Even when I wander far away from him, God loves me.
Even though I don't understand why he would, God loves me.

When I feel that I don't measure up, when I have fallen short, when I think that I should be last on the list of people accepted by God I have to come back to this prayer that Jesus gave us. I have to be reminded that God loves me like he loves his only son.

> *"I do not call you slaves anymore, because a slave doesn't know what his master is doing. I have called you friends, because I have made known to you everything I have heard from My Father."* (John 15:15 HCSB)

Here is God's invitation through Jesus: God loves us as much as he loves Jesus. We are no longer outsiders. Slaves. Servants. But now, now we are called into the inner circle. Every message from God to Jesus is made known.

But you say, "Wait a minute, I don't know everything! I don't know how my life is going to turn out, or who will win the World Series this year." Those things are not included in the message. The message is the Gospel of Jesus. The message is salvation through simple child-like faith. The message is that we are no longer enslaved to fear because we are the children of God. The message is that our God crushed death - owns it. Death went 0-1 against God and there will be no rematch.

The message is an empty tomb, a risen Savior…all because of God's love for you.

Please know that I write this as a message to myself, first, and to you, second. I write this to remind myself of God's love for me in the moments when I feel alone, abandoned, or crushed. This is not an "I have it all together" kind of message. In my pain and suffering I know of no other place to run to than to the love of God. He has yet to fail me.

"*Father, we ask you now to help us understand how much you love us, especially when we feel unlovable. Through our faith in you help us to understand how high, how wide, and how deep your love is for us. Thank you that your love is everlasting to everlasting, and that you love us as much as you love your son, Jesus, in whose name we pray, amen.*"

MOVE ON FROM THE PAST

Are you looking for an answer of how to move on from your past? I have been. I've been trying to reconcile my past with how God sees me and what God thinks of me. This past Sunday he showed me the answer to my past.

There are times when worship causes someone to realize something God has been trying to say or has been saying, but we missed it for a long time. When these moments occur they are unexpected, and the realization that washed over me on Sunday morning as I stood singing was almost overwhelming. Let me explain.

I could write a very long list of people that I have offended in my past. I've attempted to apologize to some, and others just don't want to hear from me ever again. I understand that. I could write pages and pages of all the things I've done wrong. The one thing I've never been able to fully wrap my brain around is God's forgiveness. How could He let go of my past when I can't? I saw something while other members of the worship team were singing the lyrics of "Here In the Presence" by Steven Furtick, Chris Brown and Mack Brock:

> "I know your past is broken
> You can move on it's over now
> Here in the presence of the Lord."

In that moment of time, here is what God showed to me:

As I was standing during the song in my mind's eye I caught a glimpse of an image. In the image I was standing with both arms and hands lifted up in worship. Behind me was a wall that I knew was there, yet I did not look at it. This wall had significance. The wall was located just behind me about an inch away. It was as if everything behind the wall was grayed out. A little explanation here: If I were to fill out a form on the Internet and I missed something, the button to continue may be "grayed out" which means it's not clickable. Hence, I cannot click on it and go back anything. This was the condition of the wall. I never tried to touch the wall, but there was no desire in my heart to turn and even look at the wall.

The wall represented my past. Why would I want to turn and look at it? All that was before me was vibrant and beautiful beyond words I could write here. I cannot begin to describe the colors and the brightness of what I was beholding. I can tell you this: I did not want to look away. Why turn around and away from the glorious display in front of me to look at a gray wall?

Here is what I believe many people need to hear from this song and can glean from the image that flashed in my mind:

"*I know your past is broken…*" You have been **identified**. You believe that you are known by your broken past. It may be abuse. It may be a failed marriage. It may be a lost job. It may be a combination of several things. The problem is that this is how you identify yourself. You identify yourself as the victim of your past and you let what happened in the past define what happens to you in your future. This is **not** how God operates. God does **not** work to remind us of our past. He works overtime to remind us of what the future can hold for us and how he sees us.

> *"For I know the plans I have for you" — this is the Lord's declaration — "plans for your welfare, not for disaster, to give you a future and a hope."* (Jeremiah 29:11 HCSB)

> *"Now this is what the Lord says — the One who created you, Jacob, and the One who formed you, Israel — "Do not fear, for I have redeemed you; I have called you by your name; you are Mine."* (Isaiah 43:1 HCSB)

God has a plan for your future. He knows what steps you will take:

> *"The very steps we take come from God; otherwise how would we know where we're going?"* (Proverbs 20:24 MSG)

God spends so much time on your future that he doesn't spend a lot of time on your past. In fact, God works hard to bury it so that you and I cannot find it again:

> *"He will again have compassion on us; He will vanquish our iniquities. You will cast all our sins into the depths of the sea."* (Micah 7:19 HCSB)

So, to recap: yes, your past is broken. Mine is, too. I have yet to meet someone whose past is not broken. Here is where the permission comes into play: "*You can move on; it's over now.*"

Use your God-given permission to stop focusing on the past

What is over now? Your past. So is mine. Your past is the gray wall. Not clickable. You cannot look back into the wall and see things clearly. Everything that is behind the wall is gray and not definable. So now, we move on.

> *"Brothers, I do not consider that I have made it my own. But one thing I do: forgetting what lies behind and straining forward to what lies ahead, I press on*

> *toward the goal for the prize of the upward call of God in Christ Jesus."* (Philippians 3:13-14 ESV)

"*You can move on; it's over now.*" Look forward from your past toward the glorious beauty that God has created for us to observe everywhere we look. Keep going away from your past toward the future God has created for you.

There are two very divergent paths that people can take. One path is defined by what happened in the past. People who are victims and who let that victimhood define them are destined to be controlled by that past. The second path is defined by who God says we are. This path requires following God, listening for his voice, spending time with him, learning more about who he is, and the plans he has for one's life.

I choose the second option.

"*Here in the presence of the Lord.*" What location do you find yourself in right now? Have you been in the presence of the Lord to experience what it is like? I must admit that there have been a couple of times when I have gone to prayer that I have covered my head because I felt as though I could not approach God any other way. There have been moments of worship that I have had where the presence of the Lord was like a mist hanging over the congregation.

You say, "Great! How can I find the presence of the Lord? Where do I go to find him so that I can experience this wonderful thing you are writing about?"

> *"You have encircled me; You have placed Your hand on me. This extraordinary knowledge is beyond me. It is lofty; I am unable to reach it.*
>
> *Where can I go to escape Your Spirit? Where can I flee from Your presence? If I go up to heaven, You are there; if I make my bed in Sheol, You are there. If I live at the eastern horizon or settle at the western limits, even*

> *there Your hand will lead me; Your right hand will hold on to me.*
>
> *If I say, "Surely the darkness will hide me, and the light around me will be night" — even the darkness is not dark to You. The night shines like the day; darkness and light are alike to You.*
>
> *For it was You who created my inward parts; You knit me together in my mother's womb. I will praise You because I have been remarkably and wonderfully made.*
>
> *Your works are wonderful, and I know this very well."* (Psalms 139:5-14 HCSB)

Where can you go? Nowhere. God comes to you. You don't have to move. The Spirit of the Lord finds us. He seeks us out.

> *"What man among you, who has one-hundred sheep and loses one of them, does not leave the ninety-nine in the open field and go after the lost one until he finds it? When he has found it, he joyfully puts it on his shoulders, and coming home, he calls his friends and neighbors together, saying to them, 'Rejoice with me, because I have found my lost sheep! ' I tell you, in the same way, there will be more joy in heaven over one sinner who repents than over ninety-nine righteous people who don't need repentance."* (Luke 15:4-7 HCSB)

There is also a promise to be found in the continuation of a verse previously quoted:

> *"For I know the plans I have for you" — this is the Lord 's declaration — "plans for your welfare, not for disaster, to give you a future and a hope. You will call to Me and come and pray to Me, and I will listen to you.* ***You will seek Me and find Me when you search for Me with all your heart.****"* (Jeremiah 29:11-13 HCSB, emphasis mine)

Wow! Think about this concept: Jesus is looking for you. He leaves the rest of flock to search everywhere for you. If you look for God with all of your heart, he promises that you will find him. My friend, no religion offers this. Entering into a relationship with the God of this universe gives us hope. Hope that we will be found and that we will find him who is Love.

Do you need help moving forward from your past? I know that you're broken. I'm broken. My heart has been repaired so many times by the loving Father who sent his son to look for us. However, being broken doesn't define you. Let God define who you are and move on from your past. The past is over. God's presence is available all the time. Be who God says you are to be and don't give any more power to the past that haunts you.

Pray this with me:

"Jesus, how desperately we need you to be present with us. We have given power to the wrong thing in our lives: our past. We have allowed things that no longer matter to define who we are. We have set out on the wrong path and we need you to correct our course of life. Show us your presence and your glory. Show us the loving Father who is always good and whose love for his children never fails. Be who you are, the Savior who will always find his lost sheep and will never stop looking for those who are lost. Be near. Show us perfect love. In your name we pray, amen."

THE MOST IMPORTANT PRAYER

I am certain that my son will never forget the moment I posed the following question to him: "What are you going to do if I died tomorrow?" I will never forget the look on his face. The look was a cross between being horrified that I would ask the question and being horrified about a reality he will one day have to face. Remove the bedrock of the family and what happens to those left behind? Do they scatter? Do they stick together? Do they systematically go off in different directions as life changes occur?

I first asked my son that question over a year ago. I remind him of the question from time to time because he has yet to give me a solid answer. How would you answer a parent or a spouse if they asked you a similar question?

Another question that I must answer is this: Have I done a more-than-adequate job of preparing my kids to live in this world without me? Or even deeper: Have I left enough of a legacy that my kids would be able to look back on my life and follow the example that I have set? As part of my legacy, faith in Jesus Christ is central. He is the center of my theology and philosophy. He is the reason I am alive. My life should reflect the Jesus that I serve so that my children will know, beyond a shadow of a doubt, that I loved and followed him.

As I contemplated the contents of this book, I realized that I had left out something important. It was as if the Spirit of God said to me, "You've shown them how to pray, but what if they don't know me?"

Dear reader, do you know who Jesus is?

I think about the men that I know. If you look at the men I count as my friends, you will find:

- The owner of a small business specializing in Internet Technology
- A commercial loan banker
- A Human Resources headhunter specializing in personality profiles
- The son of a former NFL player, who is the Varsity and Junior Varsity football coach for a Christian school
- A minister of music and worship in a Southern Baptist church
- A minister to children in a Southern Baptist church
- A part-time Associate Pastor, who is also a full-time roofing contractor
- The Chief Executive Officer of an independent insurance company
- The pastor of a Bible church, who also works at *Mathnasium*

They know me. These are the guys I talk to about life. I talk to them about what is happening in my daily walk and they talk to me about their lives. Our circles are intertwined, and the iron of our lives sharpens against each other in the friction of daily living. Nothing about any of us compares to what is known about Jesus Christ, the Savior of the world.

Jesus:

- Was born of a virgin, as prophesied in the Old Testament (Isaiah 7:14)
- Was raised in the Jewish town of Nazareth in Israel (Luke 1:26)

- Healed the sick (Mark 1:29-34)
- Made the blind to see (John 9:1-12)
- Walked on the water (John 6:19)
- Told a storm to stop and the elements obeyed (Mark 4:39)
- Cast out demons possessing a living human (Matthew 8:16)
- Brought the dead back to life (Luke 8:54-55)
- Was beaten by Roman soldiers (Mark 15:18-19)
- Received 39 lashes from a "Cat of Nine Tails" (John 19:1)
- Was nailed to a cross and died on that same cross (Mark 15:25)
- Was buried in a borrowed tomb (John 19:38-42)
- Was raised back to life by the resurrecting power of God (Mark 16:1-6)
- Was seen by over five-hundred witnesses (1 Corinthians 15:6)
- Ate with his followers after coming back from the dead (Luke 24:41)
- Promised to come back the same way he left the earth (Matthew 26:64)
- Is alive and well today (Revelation 1:18)

Do you know him?
Why should you know who Jesus is? The Bible is clear:

> "Jesus told him, "I am the way, the truth, and the life. No one comes to the Father except through Me." (John 14:6 HCSB)

> "I am the way, the truth, and the life. No one comes to the Father except through Me."

> "For all have sinned and fall short of the glory of God." (Romans 3:23)

> "If we say we have no sin, we deceive ourselves, and the truth is not in us." (1 John 1:8 ESV)
>
> "For our sake he made him to be sin who knew no sin, so that in him we might become the righteousness of God." (2 Corinthians 5:21 ESV)
>
> "For by grace you have been saved through faith. And this is not your own doing; it is the gift of God, not a result of works, so that no one may boast." (Ephesians 2:8-9 ESV)
>
> "For we conclude that a man is justified by faith apart from the works of the law." (Romans 3:28 HCSB)

This is, by no means, an exhaustive list of all of the Scriptures pointing to who Jesus is, but I feel that they are important to point out to people who may not know him.

If you have lived a life of never crossing the threshold of a church, these verses are for you. If you were forced into a religion as a child, these verses are for you. If you have been jaded against Christianity because of the people of your local church who did not resemble the Jesus who offers grace, mercy, and forgiveness for free, these verses are for you. If you made an emotionally-charged decision at youth camp but have never done anything to have an actual relationship with Jesus Christ, these verses are for you. No matter your situation, these verses are for you.

The most important thing you can do in your life is to come to the realization that without the Author of Life, you have no life. Without the one who created Hope, you have no hope. Without a relationship with the One who forgives, you cannot begin to forgive yourself.

The single most important, simple prayer you can ever pray is the prayer asking Jesus to be the Lord of your life, to forgive you of your sins, and to accept the free gift of grace that he offers to you right now as you read these words.

If you are reading this book and don't know Jesus as Savior, I encourage you to pray the most important prayer in this book. Your life will never be the same.

Jesus, I come to you today to admit that I am a sinner. I admit that I cannot live without you and I need a savior. I turn from my sins and ask that you forgive me today, right here, right now, and create in me a clean heart. Give me new your life that is abundant and free. I accept your gift of salvation. I accept your mercy and grace. Come and live within me, change my life, and lead me all the rest of my days. I give my life to you. Thank you for loving me. Help me to learn to love you in return. In your name I pray, amen.

If you have prayed this prayer for the first time, congratulations on your entrance into the kingdom of Heaven! The next step is to tell someone! Contact a local Bible-believing church and tell them that you have prayed this prayer for the first time. They will be able to help you begin your relational journey with the One who made you and loves you beyond your wildest imagination.

This decision that you have made is life-changing. I promise that you will never regret praying this prayer, and God will never fail you.

Pray simple prayers. The Father loves you and listens to every word.

WHERE IT ALL BEGAN

The real genesis for this book began long before I typed out my first article for Prayer Igniters. All of this started with my preparations for my second trip to Romania in 2007. Having one international trip under my belt from the year prior, I was in a different frame of mind as I prepared to go back overseas.

My preparations were different because I was more spiritually focused about everything. I felt led by the Holy Spirit to sit down one evening in the spring of 2007 to write on a legal pad. What I wrote on the legal pad was every sin that I could think of that I had committed against God but had not asked forgiveness for. I had taken the steps to make sure that my will was updated before I left, and now I wanted to make sure my relationship with God was updated as well. I remember praying over the list I had created. I asked for forgiveness for everything listed and in the end I found myself face down on the floor.

I felt the presence of God in that room. I was face down not wanting to move because I didn't want his presence to leave. I didn't speak for the same reason. I felt like I had said enough.

The very next day I talked with my friend, Jeremy Edgar, and told him what I had done and experienced. I told him about the list and his response was, "Burn it." Those sins were confessed and forgiven. There was no reason to keep them around.

The story doesn't end here.

One of the things I had been praying for most of 2006 and into

2007 was that God would provide for me someone to marry. I had been specific with God. I was praying for:

- Someone who would love me for who I was and was not interested in trying to change me.
- Someone who would love my children like I loved them.
- Someone who would help me in caring for them and raising them to be followers of Christ.
- Someone who would be a wife to me and not shut me out in any way.

I had finally allowed myself to read Ephesians chapter five and God was working on my heart to be ready to live out the twenty-fifth verse of that chapter:

> *"Husbands, love your wives as Christ loved the church, and gave his life up for her."* (Ephesians 5:25 NIV)

This is a monumental task. This is more than being the "man of the house." This verse is loaded with responsibility and expectations. Loving your wife as Christ loved the church. That's a tough act to follow. Only the agape love of Christ makes this task possible.

I prayed for a wife. I prayed for forgiveness and had prepared to fly to Romania for a mission trip. I was right where I needed to be, even though I had told everyone close to me that I was finished with dating. God wasn't finished.

Smack in the middle of the effort to get myself ready for the Romania trip I made a realization about myself: I was done with the rollercoaster of emotions that went with dating. I was done with having to deal with someone else's crazy. I did not like the current dating scene, nor the games that people played in dating. I told all my friends I was done. No more dating.

God had me right where he wanted me.

After arriving in Romania at Camp Integro outside of Lunca

Bradului, I was introduced to the rest of the team already in Romania that consisted of four interns who had been in country for three weeks. This was their last week. One of the four women in the group of interns was a single, never married, teacher from Baltimore. Kelly was unlike anyone I had ever met before. I could spend the next forty pages talking about her, but what drew me to Kelly was her smile and her heart for the children we were working with.

Kelly and I were put together for the rest of the week out on the soccer field because I was the youngest member of my mission team and Kelly was a high school and college field hockey player. In between the groups that came out to play games, Kelly and I played Kelly's favorite game: One-thousand questions. We got to know a lot about each other. I discovered that there was a nine-year difference in age between us. When we first met, I had surmised that there was more of an age difference. Age wound up not being a deterrent to our relationship. I answered Kelly's questions with much honesty. I gave her all the information about me and my situation. I told her about my kids. I told her about the divorce. I told her about my current life situation and all of the details that went with it. She didn't flinch, but listened to everything I had to say.

On Wednesday of that week Kelly and I were taking a group of kids up the stairs to the mess hall for lunch. As we were walking up the stairs a voice from behind me said, "*That one.*"

I looked around for who had spoken to me. All around me were Romanian orphans. No one old enough to have that deep of voice was around me. I looked back at Kelly. Well, just her calves. She was ahead of me on the stairs and that's all I saw of her. In Romania, sometimes a staircase resembles a ladder.

In my own head I said to the voice: "That one?"

The voice: "*That one.*"

Me: "That one. Really?"

The voice: "*That one.*"

This was the second time in my life that I had heard the voice of God audibly. He had answered my prayer and Kelly's.

You see Kelly's prayer for many years was for a husband that would fit the following description:

- Loved God
- Loved music
- Blonde hair
- Blue eyes
- Shared her political views

I was the actual answer to Kelly's prayer. Think about that. Kelly's prayer was not "God find me a husband," but rather "God I'm looking for this particular guy." This should be an encouragement to everyone to pray specifically, because God does answer specifically.

When we got back to the United States and I got over my jet lag, I gave Kelly a call. I had acquired her phone number thirty seconds before she got on the plane for Baltimore. No, really, it took me twenty minutes to work up twenty seconds of courage to get her phone number. My good friend and mentor, John Frank Reeve, who was leading this trip, even called me while we were in the airport and told me to get Kelly's phone number. John Frank was at one gate and I was at Kelly's departure gate. He was prodding me towards this relationship because he had seen that we were good together.

I made the call two days after arriving back in Texas and shocked her. Kelly thought this was another mission trip friendship that really wouldn't go anywhere, and it was flattering for me to fawn over her. But really? She was on the east coast and I was in God's country - Texas. This wouldn't work. Or would it?

Kelly and I dated long distance for five months before becoming engaged in December of 2007. I had endured several trips to Baltimore that were "Come and Meet Kelly's Boyfriend" nights where I was grilled beyond imagination by Kelly's friends. I took their questions and gave my best answers. Some were personal and some were theological. It was a good exercise for me because I had to speak out loud about my faith and put into words what I believed.

I also won over her mom. Little did I realize I was about to be awarded the best mother-in-law in the world. I also hit the jackpot with extended family that would help me grow into becoming who God was calling me to be.

In July of 2008, Kelly and I were married on a beach in Florida. That was another miracle; the day of the wedding, planned for outside on the beach, the sky poured buckets of water. But God broke up the low-pressure system over Tampa Bay that day, even though weather forecasters said it would rain the rest of the week. He created an incredible backdrop for our wedding and wedding photos. Our friends collected seashells from the beach and created a seashell walk way for Kelly to walk down and a seashell heart for us to stand in as we declared to all present that we had chosen each other for the rest of our days on this earth.

That's how God had a girl from Baltimore meet a guy from Texas while we were in Romania, and who married one year later on a beach in Florida before settling in Texas.

When I sit and ponder about who God is and what he does and does not do, all I need to do is reflect on this story to see how God does indeed answer our prayers. In his infinite love, mercy, and grace he answers the cry of our hearts because he is our loving Father. I see his answer to my prayer every day when I look at my wife. I see his answer in the home that we purchased. I see his answer in the evening sunsets he paints and the beauty of nature we observe on the trails we walk.

God loves to hear from his children. He wants to hear from you.

In closing let me leave you with the words that James Robison spoke that burned themselves into my heart. I hope they are a source of comfort: "The Father loves you."

Printed in the United States
By Bookmasters